A CHILD OF WAR

EWA REID-HAMMER

Contents

Suffering is part of human experience. This book is dedicated to everyone searching to heal the pain, and to those who have supported me, especially my sister, Helen.

Introduction

At the center of my existence, in a place I am always very reluctant to visit, there is a deep dark lake of sorrow, despair, anguish, pain, loss. It was there from the very beginning and I lived at its edge until my early twenties when I read a book on Reality Therapy. This book told me that I didn't have to live with my pain, that I could choose to be happy instead. I made a conscious rational decision to do so and was able to cut off completely for many years from that place. I truly believed that I had left it behind forever and had moved ahead in a positive way. It took a long time to realize that I had never left at all, that it was always with me, a part of me. That totally out of my conscious awareness, it continued to affect and influence every aspect of my life: my thoughts, feelings, actions and relationships with others.

As a young child, I slept with a sharp knife under my pillow. I knew I was not strong enough to kill an attacker, but I could kill myself, thus avoiding unbearable torture and pain. This made me feel safe, gave me a sense of control over my fate.

I learned young that nothing lasted so that it made no sense to attach myself. Parents would leave, home and possessions would have to be abandoned. And I knew by the time I was two years old, that neither parents nor other adults have the power to protect themselves or me from being hurt, to keep me safe.

In the past, I never wanted to share these memories. In time, I have become aware to what extent I was affected, and my life shaped by the war and its aftermath. Even though these experiences were not understood at the time, and are only partially consciously remembered, they have had a determining impact on my personality, relationships and life. I think that such impact is often misunderstood and underestimated in the case of adults, but especially in that of children. I want to explore the long-term effects war experiences have on lives that have been scorched by them. I want to share with others the fact that in the words of Oliver Wendell Holmes: "In our youth, our lives were touched by fire". Though we may try, as I did for years, we can never leave that past behind or exorcise it. It is with us forever. Perhaps, we can come to terms with it by understanding and sharing that insight with others.

"For perhaps we are like stones; our own history and the history of the world embedded in us, we hold a sorrow deep within and cannot weep until that history is sung." (Susan Griffin: "A Chorus of Stones")

Telling the story, especially in writing, has the effect of shining a spotlight on the past, illuminating its dark corners and revealing its hidden meaning. This leads to a new and different, possibly liberating perspective on events that until now have been a fossilized memory of undifferentiated pain.

This is the story of a very frightened, traumatized child, who grew up to be a frightened, traumatized adult, and her journey from Good Friday, a place of suffering and death, to Easter Sunday, the place of new meaning-new life.

As Matthew Fox wrote: "Good Friday rules for a short period. But the longer period is the new life and the victory over death and the fear of death that Easter Sunday represents. It is that hope that rises daily with every new sun. Moving beyond the fear of death we can live fully again and cease our immortality projects, our empire building and pyramid constructing (wall street too) and get on with... living. Which is sharing. Now our fear of death does not have to rule our lives. Now we can live fully, generously and creatively."

The trauma of violence, which surrounds us and to which we are a helpless witness, creates a mysterious and hidden wound. It is hard to understand and accept; it is easier to deny. Others, trying to be helpful and puzzled by your pain will say: Nothing so terrible actually happened to you, get over it", and you yourself will deny the effects following the exhortations of friends to let go of the past, to move on. But acknowledged or not, the festering wound remains unhealed, deep within the psyche wreaking damage and devastation on the inner land-scape. In the outer world it is expressed by paralysis, an inability to take risks or express creativity, a rigidity and refusal to open to life. The inner kingdom lies a fallow wasteland. It is the wound of the Fisher King and it awaits a knight in search of the Grail who knows the right question, in order for it to be healed.

The quest is the psycho-spiritual journey undertaken with the goal of achieving an inner balance between the inner world and outer one in which we live. The knight is one who accepts the challenge of the quest, which is fraught with many dangers. It can be refused, but once accepted there is no way back. It must be seen through to the end. If successful, the hero returns home with a precious gift for the community.

The trauma of violence causes an existential wound, but what is the nature of this wound, and what is the question that can heal it?

Survivors of an epic trauma have a mission to never forget, to keep it alive in their own consciousness and that of the world so that it will never again be allowed to happen. We feel we owe this to the victims who did not survive, and to future generations.

It is important to make sure such events are not forgotten. When, however, we identify with them they start distorting our very being in fundamental ways, so that in the end we ourselves become that which we condemn, despise and deplore. There is a way of remembering and honoring the past without turning it into a present, which distorts history and human lives.

My story is the journey from trauma, which left me with a false identity, through anger, depression, terror and denial, finally to a transformative understanding, which allowed me to find the meaning of my experience. War is not the only cause of trauma. In fact, my deeper trauma came not from the war itself, which I was too young to understand and fully experience, but rather from its aftermath: the wounds sustained by my parents and those around me, which unhealed distorted their life and mine. Trauma does not always look dramatic from the outside. It is what happens to the victim on the inside that matters.

I had worked with or known many people, who experienced despair rooted in past trauma, and unrelated to their present life. The trauma could have happened recently or many years ago. It could have been a single unexpected, horrific event shattering a person like a bomb, or a

sequence of ongoing, painful or frightening events like indoctrination or solitary confinement, for example, which in time wear away a person's identity and corrode their soul.

Or, it could have been a sequence of smaller wounds inflicted with regularity so they never heal, so that even though each in itself is not life threatening, over a period of time they can cause death from loss of blood.

Trauma can be a combination of both acute and chronic events, and it can happen to a single individual, to entire communities. Persecution for political, religious, ethnic or other reasons, such as the attempted extermination of Jews by Hitler, or of Kurds by Saddam Hussein, of Tutsis by Hutus or of Armenians by Turks to name just a few of a long list of genocides, traumatizes entire peoples. War traumatizes entire nations.

A single violent event like an exploding bomb, sends shock waves that kill or maim all those in its perimeter, and have a profound negative and often lasting effect all those connected to the victims: family, friends, community, even strangers. The soldier returning from Iraq with PTSD, suffering a breakdown and shooting ten people in the public square, has not only destroyed himself and his family but also the ten strangers he shot. He has had a traumatizing effect on the entire community.

Less dramatic but equally painful is the destruction of an individual, and the aftereffects on all those who loved him. The Vets who come home unable to connect emotionally with friends or family, unable to adjust to civilian life, unable to get over the rage and alienation which form the everyday fabric of their life are not only unable to move on to a brighter future, but cannot help contaminating anyone they touch with their anger and despair.

Effects of trauma are as varied as the people subjected to it. They depend on the person, the severity of the trauma and circumstances during and after. The effects are often physical, though not always easily connected with the trauma. They are always psychological. A person undergoing frightening and incredibly painful experiences must erect defenses that will enable him/her to survive. Once the threat is removed, these life-saving defenses, no longer needed, actually get in the way of moving ahead in life, but they become difficult to abandon. There is also the inevitable fact of viewing life thereafter through the lens of trauma. Intimate relationships are distorted or destroyed, and there is a negative impact on career and creativity.

Shockwaves of a broken life reverberate through the family and community.

The following two stories come from books, but they reflect the experience of thousands upon thousands of victims of war and violence. They demonstrate the possibility of healing.

Unbroken: A WWII story of Survival, Resilience and Redemption, by Laura Hillenbrand.

Zamperini's bomber was shot down in the Pacific and he survived for days in a life raft with no food or water and despite shark attacks and shootings from a Japanese gunboat. Finally captured, he then experienced the beatings and torture, the starvation rations and terrible living conditions in a Japanese POW camp.

After the end of the War, he returned to the States and married, but quickly descended into a desperate spiral of alcohol and anger that threatened his marriage and his life. Miraculously, after connecting with Billy Graham he was able to let go of his anger and desire for revenge. He stopped drinking and became an inspirational speaker and advocate for troubled youths.

I Shall Not Hate: A Gaza Doctor's Journey on the Road to Peace and Human Dignity, by
Dr. Izzeldin Abuelaish.

As the eldest son having to care for his family because of his father's illness, the author had a childhood of hardship and starvation in a poor refugee village in Gaza, after the family was forced off their land in Israel. Despite all odds, he became a doctor and the first Palestinian to work in an Israeli hospital forging close links with colleagues. While living in a refugee camp in Gaza, with no opportunities for his children, the daily humiliation of crossing into Israel for work, he lost his wife to leukemia, and then lost 3 of his daughters when the Israelis fired into his home in the Gaza strip. His daughters died simply because they had been sleeping against "the wrong wall" that evening. Despite these tragic events, he refuses to hate and continues to work for peace between the two peoples.

We all know of Nelson Mandela, who spent over thirty years in prison because of his opposition to Apartheid, before winning the Nobel Peace Prize in 1993, and being inaugurated as the first democratically elected president of South Africa. Not embittered by his suffering, he was able to lead his country forward toward healing its wounds.

The Dalai Lama lost his country and helplessly watched for years it being devastated and his people being tortured and killed. He has spent his life in exile. Yet he refuses to preach hatred against the oppressors and continues to call for peace and understanding.

How did these people do it? How did they transform feelings of anger and hate, the understandable desire for revenge, into feelings and actions that were healing for them and all those around them? How did they move from alienation to connection?

Transformation can happen in many different ways including spiritual/religious epiphany, art/music, or good works. It is the process of moving away from the past of an impotent victim of trauma, to the future of a survivor, who can not only move ahead creatively through life, but having been in hell, guide others out of the abyss. There is a different, better way to handle suffering. *The scars can become a testament to experience, courage and healing instead of a focus for endless suffering.*

My own journey from trauma is the story of transforming the fear and pain into understanding and forgiveness. My painful experiences became understood as a necessary, if difficult, preparation for my mission in life and for helping me develop into who I truly am, my real self. The process was an inward re-orientation from 'Me' and my pain, to the 'Other', and his/her suffering. As a result, I became able to find and pursue a path of service, which gave meaning to my life, and which freed me from the demons of my past. Nothing is perfect and I still have a long way to go. But I am on the right path.

My goal in writing this book was to provide hope, encouragement and some guideposts for all those on the difficult journey of healing.

The Nightmare

ONE

The War

PEOPLE NEED CERTAIN THINGS TO GIVE THEM PSYCHOLOGICAL grounding and stability. Loss of love, peace, feelings of safety, or one's home causes trauma. Trauma leaves scars.

In my case, everything was lost.

In the fall of 1939, Germany invaded Poland. I was born three years later, in Nazi occupied Warsaw. My parents and extended family stayed at the time in a large apartment building belonging to my grandparents in the heart of the capital. Before the war, my grandparents had used it as a *pied-a-terre*, where they stayed when they had business in town, or for the social events of the winter season. The rest of the time, they resided on their four thousand acre estate, about sixty miles from the city, which in the pre-war days of horse-drawn carriages was a long ride. On the estate was located my grandfather's sugar beet plantation and sugar producing plant. Four hundred acres of woods and parkland surrounded a small twenty-eight room manor and lake. There, my Grandmother presided over staff, family and children. It was there that my Father grew up with his younger brother and three sisters.

By the time I was born, the world of their childhood had been taken over by the invader, and my family had taken up residence in Warsaw. Gone was the power and control my Grandfather, a wealthy landowner and industrialist, exercised before the war. Gone was the free and easy lifestyle he and the family had enjoyed. Their entire life was now circumscribed by nightly curfews and threatened by random street roundups, arrests and executions. Grandfather was forced by the Germans to continue overseeing the sugar production from his plant, and was required to ship by rail all of the product to the German army. They did not know that he did his bit for the resistance by diverting every fourth bag to them. Sugar was a scarce and valuable commodity during the occupation and it could easily be sold on the black market with the money going toward the purchase of weapons for the underground army. Discovery of this 'subversive' act would have meant instant death for my Grandfather and his assistants.

Now, they all resided on a permanent basis in the family owned Warsaw apartment building. The large, ground-floor apartment was occupied by my grandparents and their help. The entire family often took meals together in their dining room. Because of the nightly curfew it was difficult and dangerous to venture out, so they whiled away the evenings in conversation and card games. The second floor contained several small bachelor pads used by my Dad and his siblings. At the time of my birth, my parents still lived in the now cramped apartment. There was no room for me, so I was shipped up with my nanny, to the third floor where my maternal grandmother lived. Although she did not like little children, finding them a noisy nuisance, since there was no other convenient place, grandmother agreed to let us move in.

I have no memories of my first year, but from stories I was later told I learned that despite the unusual circumstances, my life was as routine and predictable as could be. My nanny took me to mother for nursing every three hours. I slept, woke, and was diapered on a strictly regular schedule, as babies in those days were. I loved my nanny who cared for me day and night and thought she was my "mommy."

When I was about twenty months old, something happened, the details of which are hazy in my mind, but the imprint of the event would be etched inside my body and nervous system.

In the summer of 1944, my life was routine and uneventful. My parents must have made a great effort to provide this semblance of normalcy in my daily existence, while the whole world around them was spinning crazily out of control on the edge of a precipice.

Every day, they faced news of imprisonment, torture and death of relatives or friends. These were not strangers, whose tragedies one heard about on the radio or read in the papers. These were people they knew and cared about, people they loved; people they grew up with or worked with under difficult and dangerous circumstances. They were often comrades in the underground resistance movement.

My Dad was an officer in the underground army. His task was to head up a unit of men, train them for action, procure and store armaments in secret caches, and be ready for the anticipated battle against the occupant. There were orders for subversive action to be executed. Attempts were made to free political prisoners. Usually, two or three men would attack the guards during a transfer to another prison or, to the Gestapo interrogation headquarters. Bombs and other explosives were used to disrupt enemy objectives. When a Gestapo agent or SS-man particularly distinguished himself for cruelty, he was targeted for execution by underground Headquarters. Collaborators and other traitors were also on the hit list, as were businesses catering to the enemy. When my Dad received an order, it was his duty to arrange for its effective execution.

To coordinate subversive activities and maintain communication between the various units and central Headquarters, it was essential to have a reliable liaison corps. Since most of the men were in the underground army, this task fell to the women, who were less conspicuous in their wanderings throughout the city. Often they were Scout Leaders and Girl Guides[1] whose pledge to serve God and Country put them in the ranks of freedom fighters. The job was extremely dangerous. When they were caught, they did not die a quick or easy death. Because their work required them to know the location and at least the pseudonyms of the general staff and the unit commanders they were delivering orders to, they faced relentless torture in the Gestapo interrogation chambers. Betraying one's comrades to certain agonizing death was the ultimate fear. They carried cyanide pills to take when they could bear no more, but sometimes the pills were found and taken away; sometimes they waited too long until it was too late. It is amazing how few of these heroic women broke and betrayed their trust. My mom was a Girl Scout Troop leader assigned to liaison duty.

Warsaw was under military occupation. Citizens had no rights. Anyone looking suspicious to any German was immediately stopped, searched and frequently hauled in for a more thorough interrogation. Because of the danger of being found with incriminating documents, liaison workers had to find creative and ingenious ways to conceal them. My mother decided that although the Nazis were exhaustive in their searches, even they would have little enthusiasm for examining a baby's dirty diapers. A thin waterproof pouch was inserted between two diapers and pinned on me. My Mom took me for a walk to visit friends. My diaper was changed in due course and the return trip home was much safer and more relaxed. When she became pregnant with my sister, especially toward the end of the pregnancy and for a few months after, my Dad was reluctant for Mom to perform her dangerous duties; so he would carry them out instead. Mom did not like him to do it. She felt that a woman with a child was less likely to be stopped by the Germans. Dad was adamant, however, and unless he was tied up by his own responsibilities he took me in my carriage with the little package securely wrapped around my behind.

As a small child, I knew nothing of all these matters. I liked the walks to the park with my beloved nanny, Danda. Her real name was Wanda, but I was just starting to talk and couldn't pronounce her name, so she became Danda. Walks with Danda were fun. We went to the park, where she sat on a bench and talked to the other nannies, while I sat in the carriage and watched older children running around and playing. Sometimes I took a nap. Danda was never in a hurry. Walks with Mom or Dad were not like that at all. We never went to the park. We always seemed to walk quickly to some strange place I didn't know. They changed my diaper and quickly walked back home. They always seemed in a hurry.

One day, my Dad took me for a walk. I was sitting up in the carriage, leaning over to see the sights. We came to a stop at a street corner, when a short way from us I saw a big man in uniform hitting an old man with a stick. The old man was lying on the ground. I did not understand what was happening and I did not know many words yet, but I *did* know the word for the bad man in uniform.

Excitedly, I leaned out as far as I could toward him, and pointing my finger shouted at the top of my lungs: *Shvab! Shvab!* (This was a pejorative name the Poles used for the enemy.)

My Father violently pushed me down inside the carriage. As I opened my mouth to scream in protest, he hissed at me: "Be quiet and don't move." There was something frightening in his voice and demeanor. The scream died in my throat. I lay quiet and motionless all the way home. I could not move my arms or legs. I could not make a sound. I was too scared to even cry.

This was the first time that violence and fear entered my short life. In subsequent years I would experience that jolt of fear again and again, piercing my body like electricity or lightning. Like that time, long ago, it would leave me paralyzed with terror. In retrospect, this was my first personal experience of the war, which would soon take center stage in my life, and which to this day remains its most defining event.

TWO

Boots

AFTER THE BIRTH OF MY SISTER, HELEN, IN APRIL OF 1944, we moved in with my parents to a larger apartment on the second floor, still in the large apartment building owned by Grandfather, but this one containing two bedrooms. The building was located in central Warsaw, on a lovely tree-lined avenue. One night, about three months later, a terrifying incident took place, one that would mark my young mind forever.

I woke with a start. It was very dark, but the night was not quiet as usual. Something was very wrong.

Heavy boots were stomping up the marble steps leading to our floor. The stillness of the night was shattered by loud banging on the front door. I started to cry, but my cries were drowned by the banging. It sounded like someone was breaking down our door.

I saw the light go on in the next room, and heard my Father moving and my baby sister crying. Soon, he came out in his dressing robe and unlocked the front door.

I heard strange, loud voices. Presently, two huge men in big boots turned on the big light in my bedroom. They looked at me, walked past the bed, and started making a big mess in my room, throwing things on the floor like two naughty kids. I hid my head under the blanket. I didn't know who they were or what they were doing, but I felt very scared. After a while, they turned the big light off and left my room. I peeked out from under my blanket. There were clothes and toys thrown all over the floor. *Danda won't like this mess*, I thought.

When they left my room, there was more talking in the hall. My room was dark, but I could partly see into the hall. The men in boots stood there, talking in a strange language I didn't understand. From my parents' room, I heard Mom's voice saying softly: "May God protect you". I didn't know what she meant. She sounded very upset. Helen was wailing again, and Mom hushed her.

My dad came out of the bedroom, all dressed. He followed the men in boots downstairs and into the street. Somehow, I knew that he didn't want to go with them, that he wanted to stay home with us.

I lay motionless, not making a sound until I was sure they were gone. Then I lay silent and still, making sure they were not coming back. I was paralyzed with fear.

Suddenly, I heard a sound I had never heard before. It came from the room next door. It took a while for me to realize that my Mother was crying. I had never heard a grownup cry before. I thought only kids cried and parents made them better. This made me even more terrified than the men in boots who took Daddy away. Everything was too scary. I shut my eyes tight and covered my head again with the blanket. But I couldn't keep out the sound of her sobs. After a long time, I fell asleep and in my dreams I heard Boots on the stairs, and my Mother crying.

The next afternoon, Daddy came back, and seemingly all was well. As was the custom, no one explained anything to the children. I'm not sure what I was capable of understanding at that stage anyway. But the terror of that night remained locked in my body. For many, many years I had nightmares of bad men in Boots coming in the night to get me.

When I was much older, I learned from my parents what really happened that night. The Gestapo was looking for a certain freedom fighter and mistakenly arrested my Father. After interrogating him, they realized he was not the man they wanted and released him. This was a miracle in itself, as usually, once someone fell into the hands of the Gestapo they did not get out so easily, if at all. Mother, knowing full well of Dad's underground activities, naturally thought they were after him, and believed she would never see him alive.

That night she lost her milk and was unable to nurse the baby again. It happened at the worst possible time, as within a couple of weeks the Warsaw uprising would begin. It would last two months, and leave us homeless. Towards the end, all food would be scarce, and that suitable for a five month old infant, especially milk, almost impossible to find. Later, Helen would develop rickets due to inadequate nutrition at that time.

THREE

Tiger Shooting

As THE GERMANS WERE BEING PRESSED ON THE WESTERN front by the Allies, Soviet troops were marching full steam across eastern Poland toward Warsaw. In the last weeks of August, it became very clear that it was they, rather than the western forces that were going to 'liberate' Warsaw. This presented a major problem for the Poles. Desperate as they were to get out from under the Nazi yoke, most of them had equal fears of a Soviet occupation. The decision was made, by leaders of the underground together with the government in exile situated in London, that Warsaw had to make a critical attempt to free itself. This, the reasoning went, would prevent the Soviets from using the guise of liberation to take over the capital and the country.

It was believed that the Allies, who had already recaptured France, would assist Warsaw by bombing German troops, and dropping ammunition and supplies to the freedom fighters. At the rate they were advancing, Soviet troops were expected to reach Warsaw within days, and help drive the Germans out. As long as the Poles started the fight, and were instrumental in liberating their own capital, they believed their independence would be secure. And so, on September 1, 1944, the Warsaw insurrection began.

As the fighting progressed, the better organized, better armed and far more numerous German forces backed up by artillery, tanks and air power, started gaining the upper hand in the bloody street by street, house by house, often hand to hand combat. Many of the resistance fighters were civilians, sometimes women and children. They were untrained, and often unarmed in the conventional sense. The underground army, with more training but with minimal arms and supplies to begin with and suffering heavy losses in manpower, were running out of ammunition as well as food. Although the British attempted to help with drops of supplies into the struggling city, they were mostly prevented by the Luftwaffe from getting in close enough to be successful. Some of the shipments fell into German hands, others burst on impact and were ruined. Very little arrived intact. The food and water situation was becoming critical for all inhabitants of Warsaw. The ammunition and weapons shortage was already critical for the fighters.

When the Soviet troops arrived across the Vistula, their help was desperately needed. The massive army, clearly visible across the river, struck hope into the hearts of the freedom fighters. The German attempts to crush Warsaw before being driven out by the Russians, appeared to be thwarted. The Allies had arrived! The Soviets marched to the river separating them from the embattled city, stopped and made camp. After a few days, it became clear to both sides that they would not cross the river to aid the Polish insurrection. The bright hope turned to despair. Everyone knew it was over.

Now the Germans had some breathing space to finish what they had always planned, the total and complete destruction of Warsaw. In addition to bombs by air, they brought in tanks and systematically, block by block leveled the buildings. These particular tanks were called 'Tigers' and made a distinctive noise easily recognizable by frightened citizens of the area, who listened and watched powerlessly as their neighborhoods were being converted into piles of rubble.

Everything was very tense at home. Daddy was gone. Everyone seemed very upset and busy. No one had time to play. We never went outside for walks anymore. Danda was always packing things. Every now and then, we would hear loud bang, bang noises coming from the outside, followed by sounds of loud crashing. I had never heard such noises before. Danda would get all excited and scream: "The Tiger is shooting, the Tiger is shooting." It was very exciting.

Sometimes, we would hear a loud piercing sound, which caused Danda to grab me and run downstairs to the cellar. Soon, the rest of the family would assemble. There were chairs for the grownups to sit on. I remember a large table. While in the cellar, we could hear whistling sounds and then terrible crashes. I was wondering what was happening outside, but Danda refused to take me for a walk to see. Sometimes, we had to wait a long time for all the crashing to stop, before we could go back upstairs to our rooms.

One day, we heard the usual sound, which signaled Danda to carry me downstairs. This time the crashing was louder than ever. The whole house was shaking and I thought it might fall down. Danda was holding me very tight. I realized that she, too, was shaking. This made me very uncomfortable; I felt I was suffocating; I couldn't breathe. I had to get away.

I wriggled out of her arms, and before she could grab me again crawled under the table. Danda dove after me, but I evaded her in the far corner. I heard Mother telling her to leave me alone. Having escaped from Danda, I felt a sense of victory and freedom.

The crashes outside resumed closer than ever and I started shouting in glee: "Tiger shooting, Tiger shooting." I did not know how to distinguish the sound of falling bombs from that of bursting tank shells, and I had no idea what either meant, but I did correctly identify that something was shooting. And since I thought I knew all there was to know, I felt very proud of myself.

I felt no threat or fear. The only thing that had made me anxious was the palpable terror of my nanny. Once away from her trembling, I was fine. This gathering in the cellar of the family represented a break in my daily routine, which was rather exciting and fun. Though the adults didn't seem to enjoy it, to me, it was a great adventure.

FOUR

Bonfire
_____

THERE WAS ANOTHER, BIGGER ADVENTURE COMING SOON. Daddy came home again, very tired and grumpy. He looked different. When I asked him to play, he said "later", in a grouchy voice. He spent a lot of time with Mother, behind the closed doors of their room. When they came out, Mother's eyes were red and puffy.

That evening, as I sat on his lap, he told me stories about bonfires. I had never seen a fire, but Dad, a brilliant storyteller, was able to make anything come alive. He made the fire sound bright, hot, and irresistible. By the end of the evening, I wanted nothing more than to see a bonfire. Dad promised to think about it.

The next morning was bright and sunny. At breakfast, Dad reminded me about the fire and asked if I still wanted to see one. I started jumping around in excitement. He had an idea, he told me. He could start a fire in the cellar for me, but we needed fuel to keep it going. The best fuel was rubber, and the only rubber thing we had to burn was my pacifier. If I agreed to burn it, I could drop it myself into the fire, because I was a big girl now. Only big people could throw things into the fire. He told me since I was such a big girl, I didn't need a pacifier anymore.

This was too exciting. I was enormously attached to my pacifier at night, and could not go to sleep without it, but had no need for it on a sunny morning. Quickly, I ran to the nursery to fetch it. As I pulled it from my bed and held it in my hand, I felt a moment of hesitation, but the fire had become a magical image in my mind. I was enchanted by it and could not give it up. I handed the pacifier to Dad.

Now he seemed to hesitate. "I'm not sure it's such a good idea," he said. "Once it's burned, it will be gone forever. We can't get another, you know. Maybe you're not big enough." He handed the pacifier back to me.

But his hesitation strengthened my resolve. I was afraid he would change his mind and I wouldn't get my bonfire after all. Of course I was a big enough to throw things into the fire. I was not a baby anymore and didn't need a pacifier. I pushed it back at him. "I want a fire!" I insisted.

Instead of carrying me like Danda, he took me by the hand, and together we solemnly descended the flight of steps into the cellar, like two companions on a mission. I had never felt more excited and proud in my whole life.

Once we were in the cellar, Dad put together some twigs of wood mixed with paper. I had never seen the wood there before, but I had no time to think of details. Dad took out a match. Then he faced me looking very grave. "I want you to understand very clearly," He said. "If you decide to do this, the pacifier will be gone. You will have to go to sleep like a big girl, without one".

This sounded like a challenge. I nodded my head.

"And one more thing," He continued. "You must promise not to cry if you miss the pacifier. Big people miss things too, but they don't cry. You must promise to be brave and not cry for it. Promises cannot be broken. Are you big enough to keep your promise?"

I nodded again.

"Then say: I promise not to cry later." He waited.

"I won't cry," I repeated solemnly.

Dad lit the match and touched it to the paper. The flames rose and the little fire made dancing shadows on the walls of the dim cellar. It was as magical as I had imagined. More so. We kept adding little twigs, until the fire was very hot. "Now!" He said, "Throw in the baby pacifier."

I was beside myself with excitement. I tossed it in missing by a few inches. He pushed it into the flames. We clapped our hands and watched it burn. "Now you are really my big girl". Dad hugged me.

But the smell of the rubber was not so good. The fire turned smoky, and slowly burned down. We went back upstairs, hand in hand: Father with his very proud little, big girl.

That night I panicked. I realized the pacifier was gone. I started to cry. Father came to my room looking very stern. "You promised not to cry. Promises must be kept. You are my big girl now. I don't want to hear anymore about the pacifier. And NO MORE CRYING." He hugged me and left the room. From then on I cried quietly, inside, so no one could hear.

When I was much older, I asked my parents about this strange episode. They explained that at that point, the Insurrection had been lost. The people had to be ready to flee and hide from the brutality of the German soldiers, who often indiscriminately killed everyone including women and children. It was essential to be quiet in such situations in order to avoid being discovered. My parents were concerned that in the chaos of flight, my pacifier would get lost and my cries could betray us to the enemy. Dad had the idea of the bonfire in order to deal with this contingency before it arose. It was very hard on a not yet two year old, but then war always is. The strategy worked, and my pacifier was one thing they didn't have to worry about in the upcoming days, which culminated in the evacuation from our city and home.

For me, it was another lesson in tightly controlling feelings and emotions. I learned that expressing my feelings was not acceptable, not tolerated and not safe. I learned that "Big girls don't cry." No matter how I really felt I was not to shed a tear. And so I learned to cry inside.

Suppression of emotions and feelings takes a lot of energy. It can lead to repression, where one stops feeling the emotion entirely, and which plays an important role in mental illness. It also can lead to a distortion of personality. In a young child, whose personality is not yet formed, suppression causes more serious damage than in an adult.

FIVE

A Train Ride to Nowhere

THE WARSAW UPRISING WAS OVER AND WE LOST. FOR SIXTY-three days, the Poles had mounted a heroic struggle to regain their city from the Germans, but finally, they ran out of food and ammunition. Large numbers of unburied bodies began to decay and contaminated drinking water was becoming a problem. There were no drugs to treat the sick and wounded, whose numbers increased daily.

Citizens using anything possible as a weapon had fought side by side with the poorly armed underground army against a professional, well equipped force. Men, women and children manned hastily erected barricades as streets turned into battle-grounds. The whole city had become a patchwork quilt of areas, controlled by one side, directly adjacent to ones controlled by the other.

Most of the fiercely contested streets lay between the sectors, and had to be traversed by Polish couriers or whoever needed to get to the other side. Sometimes a sector was lost to the enemy, and all the combatants had to immediately get across to another friendly one in order to escape capture.

It was in such a street battle that my father's seventeen-year old brother was wounded. The Germans occupied the buildings on one side of the street; the Poles held the other. There was a steady barrage of fire back and forth. My uncle, carrying messages for a Polish unit in another sector, had to get to the other side. He got caught in the crossfire, and lay bleeding in the street wounded in both legs. Fortunately, he was able to crawl out of the direct line of enemy fire. Unfortunately, he could not get back to safety, and the Germans kept up the shooting, making rescue impossible.

A message was sent to my Dad that his brother was wounded, and he gathered three friends who agreed to help in what looked like a suicidal mission. They could do nothing until dark, when they hoped the shooting would abate. But the Germans anticipated a rescue attempt and kept up the fire. Dad knew his brother could not last much longer and that this would be their only chance. It was a tricky business, requiring steady nerves and a lot of courage. My uncle, who had lain bleeding for several hours was barely conscious. They had to get him on a stretcher and carry him back while under constant German fire. It was a miracle that they were able to do so, and more of a miracle still, that he survived.

I knew nothing, at the time, of all this. What I did sense was a pervading tension in all the adults around me. The trips to the cellar became more frequent and less fun, as the general anxiety and fear increased. I knew something bad and scary was about to happen.

It was the beginning of October 1944, and Warsaw had surrendered. Over 200,000 citizens were being herded out of the city to concentration or forced labor camps. I don't remember how it started, and there is no one left who was with us on that last day, when we were forced to leave our home, before it and our city were razed to the ground.

My clear recollections start with being carried by Dad for a long time down streets filled with rubble. Mom was carrying five-month old, baby Helen, and Danda was with us as well. We followed a long stream of people carrying children and whatever possessions they could. On the way I saw strange sights: furniture and broken stuff lying in the open, burned out houses without roofs and walls, motionless people lying in heaps by the side of the street, and people moaning or calling for help sitting or lying on sidewalks. I asked Dad why they were crying, and he said because they were hurt.

I felt scared and didn't ask any more questions. I knew full well by this time that expressing feelings was dangerous so I kept quiet despite the fear. I no longer looked to a parent for reassurance and comfort. I was getting more practice in suppressing emotion.

We walked for what seemed a very long time, when the line began to tighten and finally stopped. Dad left me with Danda and Mom. He returned shortly and after speaking to them, took me and dropped back in the line, leaving Mom with Helen way ahead. Danda gave me a teary kiss and moved away from us. I started crying. "Be quiet," Dad told me firmly. "I want Danda," I continued to wail. "If you keep crying, they will take you away," he said, and somehow I knew he meant it. I also knew 'they' were the bad guys who shot and hurt people. Now I was really frightened and remained quiet.

Slowly the line inched up toward a group of German soldiers. Behind them I saw a train. The soldiers asked Dad some questions, then pointed us to the train. We had to push our way in as the car was quite full. More people pushed in behind us. We were being crushed from all sides and I began to cry. I heard someone calling Dad's name. It was Mom with Helen in her arms, trying to push her way through the crowd to our side. Dad started pushing toward her and finally we were together.

I heard a loud bang and the light grew dim. The doors of the car had been slammed shut. The windows were very small and high up, not letting in much light. After the door closed, people spread out as much as they could. There were no seats in this train, but there was a wide shelf near where we were standing, and Dad slowly pushed close to it. People were sitting or leaning on it but he was able to get a place for Mom to sit, and a spot for me to stand on.

Mom and Dad seemed relieved to have found each other, but I wasn't happy at all. It was hot and the car smelled bad. "I don't want to be here, I complained, "I want to go home". Mom hugged me. "We can't go home now," She said. "I have to go pipi." Dad took me off the shelf, pulled off my panties and stood me on the floor. I stared at all the strangers pressing in around me. "Not here, on the potty," I whispered. "There is no potty, you have to go here." I stood for a while unbelieving. Finally, unable to hold back any longer, I let go. A stream of yellow puddled at my feet and wet my shoes. The train shuddered and started to roll. I lost my balance but the people on all sides were packed in so close that there was no room to fall. I started crying again. Dad picked me up and sat me between Mom and a big, fat old lady. I was hungry, thirsty and exhausted, but mostly scared. I just didn't understand where we were or why my parents brought us to this terrible place. Finally, I went to sleep.

I woke up screaming. I couldn't breathe. I felt a heavy thing pressing over my head and suffocating me. Dad extricated me from the fat lady who had dozed off and rolled over on top of me. I was hysterical and Dad held me. Mom was still holding Helen. I cried for my Danda, but she was nowhere in sight. I could not know that I would never see her again.

The train rattled on and on, sometimes stopping, but never letting us out. Darkness followed light and after a while I fell into a stupor no longer knowing whether it was day or night. Sometimes, I got food or water, other times I was hungry. I no longer cried. Mom and Dad seemed very tired. I slept on and off in a strange twilight zone and don't remember much.

After what seemed like an eternity, the train came to a complete stop. The sudden silence let us know the engine had been turned off. We had arrived somewhere. I woke and threw up. The car smelled worse than anything I had ever smelled in my life. I was thirsty and my mouth was dry. People were moving, waiting for the door to open, but that took a very long time-another ten hours (I was later told).

Finally, we heard the clanging of metal hinges and the doors swung open. Everyone started pushing forward, trying to get out. Dad held us back.

"I want to get out of here," I wailed.

"We will, but we don't want to get crushed," Dad told me. He was holding me in his arms again, and eventually we got to the exit.

I saw a big empty field with nothing else in sight.

"Where is our house?" I cried, "There are no houses here."

"We'll find it, don't worry." Dad sounded sure and I felt better. Wherever we were, I was happy to be off that awful train.

"I don't like trains," I announced to no one in particular.

These events had major impacts on my life. So much had happened to this little psyche. I had been exposed to events that would be traumatic for anyone at any age. A child so young could have no resources to cope with them. I had learned that it was dangerous to express emotions, and it was painful to feel them. I was becoming better and better at suppressing those feelings I could not repress. I cried inside a lot. Also, the world was becoming divided into the "good" people, who would not kill you, and the "bad" people, who probably would. Much later I would learn that this black-and-white thinking is known as a defense mechanism called "splitting." The world becomes black and white lacking the nuanced shades of gray, which actually compose most of reality.

Events themselves were engulfing us in a way that would haunt my family forever. We could not know it then, but my parents and their friends were becoming trapped in the past.[1]

SIX

New Nannies

ARRIVING IN THE SMALL VILLAGE, WE MOVED INTO A TINY
cottage. I don't remember much about the village except that
other aunts and uncles were there, also living in little cottages.

We visited uncle Zbig every day. He always lay in a white
bed, with white sheets and blankets. His legs were wrapped in
white bandages. "Why doesn't he get up?" I asked Dad. "He
can't walk," Dad answered, "The soldiers shot his legs." I
wondered if he would always stay in bed.

I wanted to go back to my house and play with my toys.
We hardly had any toys here. Most of all, I knew my Danda
was waiting for me at home, and I badly missed her. Mom and
Dad were busy. My sister and I were looked after by a strange
woman. I pestered my parents about going home, but was told
we couldn't go back yet. Soon, they would say. I never understood the explanation, or perhaps there never was one, as
parents at that time did not feel it necessary to explain things
to children.

We lived in this small village for several months in an
almost surreal situation. We had lost our beautiful home, were
removed from familiar surroundings, and lived on a day-to-
day basis until it would be possible to go back to the ruined

26

city. Tying to provide a buffer for us, my parents acted as if these highly abnormal circumstances were not unusual. They sheltered me and my sister from the traumatized refugees, who had been strangers and now were our neighbors. Their pretense at normality in this extremely abnormal situation added to the atmosphere of unreality in which we lived.

Today, we would have had community therapy in this appalling situation. We were all traumatized, displaced persons, who after having been subjected to unspeakable trauma, ended up losing their homes and possessions. Their entire lives had been destroyed. Careers, education, work all disappeared into a dark void and no longer had any meaning. Some people were physically wounded. Most had no idea, and no way to find out, where their loved ones were, or if they had survived. Some people had gone over the edge and lost control. Others were only shell-shocked, suffering what we now call Post Traumatic Stress Disorder. They were all the walking wounded.

Finally, after many months, the big day came and we went home to Warsaw. I ran into the house calling, "Danda, Danda." But she didn't come out to greet me, and after running through all the rooms I did not find her. The disappointment was too much, and I started to cry. "Danda is not back yet," Mom told me, "You have to be patient and wait." "When will she be back? Where is she?" I wanted to know. "We're not sure," was the answer.

Somewhere about that time, a tiny baby was brought to the nursery for Helen and me to see. "This is your new sister, Anne," we were told. We weren't impressed. She didn't look like much fun and was too little to play. She had her own nurse and we only saw her occasionally. We weren't allowed to touch her.

Helen and I played and ate together in our own nursery, and slept in our own bedroom. In the mornings, we were taken to visit with Grandma downstairs for a while, and Mom and Dad visited briefly in our nursery. After lunch, if the weather was nice we played outside. I had a beautiful cream colored doll carriage trimmed with chrome, a gift from Grandpa to his oldest granddaughter. At five o'clock, Dad came to the nursery to play with us. He would read us stories or watch me make towers from blocks, or help me write letters with my crayons. His visits were always fun. Mom came too, but I don't remember what we did with her.

One day, a young woman was brought to the playroom by Mom, and introduced as our new nanny. "I don't want a new nanny," I told Mom, "I want Danda."

"Danda is not here and you must listen to your new nanny," Mom insisted firmly.

This was unbearable. Not only was Danda gone, but some stranger was about to take her place. I would never let that happen. I would wait for Danda no matter how long it took. I let the woman know she was an intruder and not my real nanny. I made her life difficult pretending not to hear her orders, or ignoring them directly. I told her I hated her.

Finally, I succeeded in making her go away.

Mother was angry and told me my bad behavior had caused her to quit. She still didn't understand that was my plan. Now, I hoped, Danda would come back.

But she didn't. Another nanny was hired instead. I started my campaign of terror once again, however, this one was harder to discourage.

One morning, as I entered the playroom, I noticed an ironing board with an iron standing on it. Nanny was nowhere about. I examined the shiny object. I knew perfectly well I wasn't allowed to touch it, but it was hard to resist. Wondering if it was hot, I placed my palm squarely on the shiny, flat surface. Immediately, I jumped away screaming and holding my burned hand. It had turned a bright red and was hurting badly. In response to my cries, the housekeeper and nanny both came running.

Mrs. Lizoniowa did the housekeeping and her husband was the gardener and maintenance man. They had been with us for a long time. She scooped me up in her arms and yelled at my nanny: "Where were you? Why weren't you keeping an eye on the child?"

She rushed me downstairs to my grandmother. My hand was soaked in cool water with a soothing powder and the doctor was summoned. Fortunately, the iron had not been very hot, and I had withdrawn my hand so quickly, no major damage had been done. Despite being reminded by Mom that I shouldn't have touched the iron, the nanny was fired. I was coddled by my grandparents for a few days. It was a most gratifying ending to my misadventure.

My paternal grandmother was tolerant and loving. One morning I was brought to her bedroom while she was still in bed. After playing on the bed for a while, I got bored and went to explore her dressing table, which was full of bottles and jars. There were many very interesting things to examine. "Be careful, don't spill anything", grandfather warned.

"Let her have fun," answered Grandma. Pretty soon a colored jar slipped out of my hands and a cloud of white powder enveloped the area settling on me and everything else in sight.

"Now look what you've done. I told you to be careful. What a mess!" Grandpa sounded very displeased. "Oh, it's just a little powder," Said Grandma, "Call Mary to clean it up." I knew she had taken my side and I would not be punished. I loved my grandmother very much. From her I got the sense of unconditional acceptance and love, which I would so desperately need in the years to come. I would need these inner strengths for what was about to come.

Grandfather was the undisputed and autocratic patriarch of the family. He was the Emperor: powerful and controlling. His approval of me as his firstborn granddaughter, gave me special status in the family. He liked me as I was, and made me feel special. From him I got a sense of grounding and importance, strength, empowerment.

I continued to mourn the loss of Danda, and hope for her return. She had been my de-facto mother from birth. She was always there to comfort me when I cried, to feed me when I was hungry and to hold me when I was sad. She did not expect me to control my feelings, and allowed me to be I could who I really was: a baby-child. I could cry, scream, throw a tantrum when angry, or laugh, sing and dance when happy. She gave me total approval and affirmation. I knew that I was special and wonderful in her eyes. I did not know then, that I had lost not only her but all her gifts forever. I would spend many years in trying to find again the unconditional love she gave me, that was so suddenly and violently lost.

The loss of Danda was the first, and foreshadowed the many losses I would experience in the near future.

When the next nanny arrived, she had been warned I would be difficult and firmness was the order of the day. That evening we had potato soup served for supper in the nursery. I did not like potato soup and decided to test the resolve of the new nanny. I refused to eat it. She tried persuasion, bribery and threats, but to no avail. I simply refused.

"A stubborn one," she said. "Well, you can just sit here until you eat it."

So I sat there until bedtime, but she wasn't beaten yet. "If you don't eat it tonight, you'll get it cold for breakfast in the morning." I didn't eat it.

True to her word she served it cold for breakfast. I still refused. She threatened to serve it again for lunch. By then nothing would make me give in.

As I sat in front of the cold soup once again at lunchtime, my Grandfather unexpectedly walked in. "What's this, cold soup for lunch?" He asked. I told him I hated potato soup and nanny wouldn't give me anything else to eat since yesterday. Grandpa was horrified and ordered lunch to be brought immediately. He asked the nanny if starving a child was her idea of discipline.

She left in a huff and once again Mom had to find a replacement.

I was a stubborn child with a strong sense of what was fair and an unwillingness to compromise on that. For some reason, being the first grandchild made me special. His approval gave me grounding. He was powerful and made me feel strong, as well.

Mother's patience was wearing thin with my nanny exploits. She let me know when the next one arrived that this was it. If I misbehaved again, I would be in big trouble. The moment of truth came at bath time. Helen and I did everything together including taking long, fun baths.

The new nanny, having been warned of my temper tantrums, and afraid she couldn't control us both in the tub at the same time, insisted we must take turns. I argued with her, telling her we were allowed to bathe together. She refused to give in and put Helen in the tub keeping me out.

All my rage at her not being Danda mixed with the sense she was being unfair. I reached out and grabbed her hair. She was holding Helen in the water and afraid to let her go. I yanked and pulled out a handful of hair. Then I grabbed for more. She screamed.

People came running and pulled me away. Mother came too, and I could see she was very angry. She told me she had had enough, and slapped my bottom hard, several times.

I had never been hit before, and though later I would be spanked by Dad, this was the first and last time Mother ever hit me. I cried bitterly from outrage and humiliation more that pain. But I knew this was the end. Mom had won and the nanny would stay. She was not so bad in the end, but I would never accept her because she wasn't Danda. And I would never forgive Danda for leaving me.

I could not know then that Danda had spent the end of

the war in a work camp in Germany. I felt very abandoned and betrayed.

Danda, my primary caregiver, had represented to me security, warmth and love. My desperate attempts to get her back represented my need to recapture the stability of an earlier era. I felt hurt and angry at what I experienced as her abandonment. These episodes reinforced for me that my anger and attempts to get my way were futile. I learned again how powerless I was to influence events. These feelings of impotent anger and frustration started to coalesce into an energetic block, which would later in life immobilize me and be a huge obstacle to motivation, making decisions and moving purposefully forward.

SEVEN

Saying Goodbye

FINDING THE RIGHT NANNY WAS AN ADDITIONAL STRAIN ON Mother, who was faced with a far more serious crisis, one that would have long-term implications for our family. Father had become critically ill.

Diagnosed with acute *agranulocytosis*, a poorly understood blood disease for which there was no known cure, he was wasting away, kept alive only by daily transfusions of blood. For many months he was unable to leave his bed, where my sisters and I visited him daily for a brief good morning and goodnight kiss. He was very pale and weak; Mother did not want us to tire him. We missed his daily visits to the nursery, where he used to play games with us and read or tell us stories, and did not understand why he could no longer do so.

I didn't understand what was happening or why. The underpinnings of my world were being continually shaken and torn apart. Losing my home after the insurrection and losing Danda at the same time were traumatic changes. Now Mom and Dad were becoming less and less available, and once again there was the feeling of tension and uncertainty in the household. I didn't understand, but I felt it keenly. At an even deeper level of the psyche, my inner world – a foundational sense of security and wellbeing -- was being shaken apart, as well.

After a year, it became clear the doctors in Warsaw could not cure my father's disease. The best specialists in the world, at the time, were in Switzerland, and that was where Mother's last hope lay. She decided to take him there for treatment. It was a fateful decision, which would split apart the family and take my parents far from country and home. Planning to leave for a few months, my mother could not know that she was destined never to return.

'Liberated' from Nazi rule by the Red Army, Poland fell under the control of Soviet Russia, and would remain so for the duration of the Cold War. The local Communist government, installed and kept in power by Soviet troops stationed in Poland took its orders from Moscow. The process of converting the country to Communism, involved the persecution and elimination of prominent pre-war families.

These people had nothing to gain and everything to lose under Communist rule. They could not be expected to willingly embrace the new ideology. In general, well educated and used to wielding power, they were considered dangerous adversaries and thus declared enemies of the state. Initially they were hunted down and arrested. Some were tried on trumped up or political charges and executed. Others were deported deep into the Soviet Union where they rotted in gulags. Still others disappeared never to be heard from again. Their family members were threatened and discriminated against. Adults could not get work, and their children were barred from higher education.

My grandfather, a wealthy landowner before the war, had to go into hiding once the communists consolidated their power. He was forced to change his name, lifestyle and looks. He dared not appear in Warsaw or anyplace where he might be recognized. For many years, he lived like a simple peasant, hiding out in a village, deep in the countryside.

Another group of Poles that were slated for obliteration were those who had taken a clear anti-Communist stance during the war. There had been two distinct parties in the Polish underground, and they had quite different ideological views. The Home Army believed that Poland could not fight on two fronts. Whether one liked Communism or not, they reasoned, since the Soviets were fighting the Germans they were, for the moment at least, our allies. The Home Army had some communist sympathizers and even party members within their ranks. The National Front (NF), on the other hand, believed that the Russians were our historical enemies looking to expand their empire, and that, given the chance, they would enslave Poland as surely as the Nazis had tried to do. The NF did not trust the Russians and refused to cooperate with any Soviet interventions. Needless to say, there were no communists within their ranks. While the Soviets after taking control, had no use for any Polish patriots and treated their supporters from the Home Army abominably, members of the NF, especially the officer corps were arrested and executed promptly.

And so threat of death loomed over us again. My Dad had been an officer in the NF. Fortunately, the names of the officers and men had been encoded, and though the communists did get the memberships rosters it took them time to decipher them all.

Although my Dad was on the wanted list as the son of a prominent family, at the time when Mother applied for permission to take him for to Switzerland, his wartime activities were not known to the authorities. The communists consented to allow Dad out of the country for three months to seek a cure. The permit, however, applied only to my parents. My sisters and I were to remain in Poland as a guarantee of their return.

Helen and I were told they were going away so Dad could get better. We had no idea where they were going or what three months meant. All I understood was that we wouldn't be seeing them anymore. Helen, eighteen months younger, probably understood less.

Since losing my beloved Danda I was unable to attach myself to any of her replacements. Even though after the BIG FIGHT with Mom, which I lost ignominiously and painfully, I stopped fighting them actively, I continued to resent their presence. During the months in Milanowek, I had become more closely bonded to Mother, and keenly felt her absence in Warsaw, where she was busy nursing Dad, and I was once again relegated to the nursery in the care of strangers. Although we lived in the same building as my grandparents, Mom and Dad were the ones who had been there continuously from the beginning and throughout the frightening times of war.

I didn't throw a tantrum, as I felt powerless to stop them from leaving us. I didn't want them to go, but I no longer believed that I could fight and win. Unable to get Danda back, I lost faith in my power to get what I want. So I kissed them goodbye -- like the good little girl I *wasn't* but was *expected to be*.

Three months is a short time for an adult, but an eternity for a little girl waiting for her parents to return. Surprisingly, I did not feel the pain of 'losing' them. The family assumed that since our young lives continued in the nursery much as before, and since our parents were never involved in constant day-to-day care, we would hardly notice their absence. They were partially correct. It wasn't that I didn't notice their absence. I did, and a small dark hole started to grow inside me. But, I was already quite adept at repressing bad feelings, and so, was not consciously aware of the pain.

EIGHT

A Skit for their Return

Life in the nursery went on much as usual, despite the absence of my parents. Every day, my cousin Andy and some other children joined Helen and me for a morning of playschool at our house. We sang songs, learned short poems, listened to stories, danced, drew, colored and played. In general we had a good time. I especially enjoyed playing with Andy, who was my age and a lot of fun.

Our parents were not part of our daily life. Before they left, we only saw them once or twice a day for relatively short periods of time. Before he fell ill, Dad might come to watch me play or read a book to me sometime in the afternoon. Other than that there was the daily good morning and good-night kiss, usually for a few minutes in their bedroom. They did not feed, wash, dress or put me to bed. After dad got so ill, we saw very little of either one. So, I did not miss them in the way children would normally miss parents, who were deeply involved in their day to day lives.

One day, after what seemed like a very long time, grandma announced that they were coming back. The nursery was all abuzz. Soon they would be back and we must prepare to welcome them home!

Our governess prepared a little skit. We all had to memorize parts. Also there were poems to recite and songs to sing. So much to learn and practice! So much fun! The pitch of excitement escalated as the date of their return drew near.

Finally, the big day arrived. Today, we were told, Mother and Father would be home. I could envision myself being held in Mother's arms and kissed by Father. The bad feeling slipped away a little. Anne was only two and didn't really understand what was going on. Helen and I couldn't wait. "Are they here yet?" We kept asking all day long. But as the morning turned to afternoon and then evening our hopes started to fade.

Our governess was reassuring: "They must be delayed. Don't worry, they'll be here first thing tomorrow."

The next morning Grandmother came to the nursery. "Are they here?" I asked, knowing the answer. If they had come back, they would have come to hug and kiss us good morning. And Grandma, always a late riser, would still be in bed. "They are delayed," Grandmother told us, "We must be patient and wait a while longer."

The old, uneasy, bad feeling crept in, and I started wondering if they were ever coming back. Life resumed in the nursery as before. And after a few weeks the excitement mounted again. We had a new date for their return. We practiced our now forgotten skit with renewed vigor. Again we were eagerly ready, and again they did not come. Again we were told they would be back soon, but I knew now Grandmother was lying. They were all lying, and like my beloved Danda who vanished without a trace, they too were never coming back. And they never did.

The repeated cycles of hope and disappointment left me with the conclusion that there is no point in hope because it will end in disappointment, that people always lie, and that no matter how much I want something I wouldn't get what I wanted. It was a reinforcement of the futility of expectations and the beginning of an emotional detachment. I started to live for each day.

NINE

Going Away

I was about five years old, when my parents went away.
Summer had gone and the leaves were falling off the trees.
The bright sunny October days were coming to an end. Soon,
November with its cold, rainy weeks would be here. I no
longer thought about my parents. I knew they were gone
forever, and it was as if a part of my mind and heart
containing memories of them had been locked off.

Helen and I played together, and talked, but never of
them. It was not by any agreement, but rather by some silent,
unspoken understanding that their names were never
mentioned between us. The rest of the family was also silent
on the subject. Not knowing what to expect, they were reluctant to raise false hopes, not knowing that nothing they could
say at that point could change my conviction that Mom and
Dad were never coming back.

No one knew the deep effect this was having, not only on
my physical being and psyche, but on my ability to trust, and
connect with other people.

I had already learned through painful disappointment,
that grownups don't tell the truth. They always lied when
something was going to hurt, like a shot. They always said it

wouldn't hurt, and it always did. They said people would come back, and they didn't. They told you everything would be all right, and it never was. One couldn't trust what they said, so I made up my own mind what to believe.

One day about a year after my parents left, Grandmother came to see us. She said that tomorrow we would be going on a little trip to the mountains. She said we were going to meet our parents.

My emotional response was flat. I did not believe her and wondered where we were really going. Helen said nothing, and we didn't talk about it.

On the morning of our departure, we were awakened earlier than usual. It was still dark. As always, we were dressed in our dresses with bows in our hair. Breakfast was hurried. As we were about to leave, I ran to our playroom, shouting: "I must say goodbye to my dollies".

"Hurry up", our governess urged, "Your Grandmother does not like to be kept waiting".

I entered the darkened room alone. The morning was peeking through the drawn curtains creating a soft light full of shadows. I gathered all my dolls, kissed them, and put them in their little beds. I covered them up with their tiny quilts so they would stay warm and comfortable. Then, I said goodbye to them forever. No one had told me so, but I knew inside, I was never coming back.

We travelled by train to a little village in the mountains. It was evening when we arrived at a small hotel. We ate supper, and exhausted by the long ride went to sleep early. Late at night I awoke to hear Grandmother crying. I had no idea where we were really going or what was going to happen tomorrow, but now I knew that whatever it was, it was going to hurt. I lay awake for a long time trembling with fear, before a fitful sleep brought me some relief.

The next day dawned bright and sunny. Things looked more cheerful in the light of the morning, and for a moment I

forgot the anxieties of the night. After breakfast, Grandmother announced we were going for a walk.

Something in her voice warned me not to trust her. I
sensed danger. I refused to go and was prepared to stage a
noisy scene in the hotel. This, I instinctively knew, was the
type of situation, with which my petite and refined Grandmother would have a very tough time coping. In the past,
discipline was enforced by nannies, then governesses, sometimes parents. Grandmother always withdrew at the first signs
of trouble. I had a well-founded confidence in my capacity to
throw a huge tantrum, the kind of behavior polite adults did
not expect from well brought up children, and which left them
shocked, not knowing how to react.

"I am not going," I said, my jaw set.

We both knew that without my governess to back her up,
Grandmother was in trouble. I was not going, and as she
could not leave me behind, she could not go either. We looked
at each other like two opponents sizing each other up. I looked
her in the eye and repeated loudly: "I am not going." I kept
looking straight at her, challenging her to the next move.

Grandmother lowered her eyes. She was silent for a
moment, then replied: "I wanted to surprise you. We are
going to buy you a puppy."

This was unexpected and put me a little off-guard. I had
wanted a puppy for as long as I could remember. A little voice
in my head whispered: "Don't trust her, she's lying." But a
louder voice shouted: "A puppy, you're going to have a
puppy."

The temptation was too great. I nodded and followed her
obediently out the door. At least my heart did; my head was
still sounding a silent warning.

We walked a distance, and finally arrived in a part of town
that looked different from any place I had ever seen. There
were no shops or nice looking houses. Everything looked gray
and a little dirty. I did not feel good being there and I started

feeling anxious again. Something was not right. We stopped in front of a rickety staircase leading to the second floor of an apartment house.

I protested: "This is not a pet store."

"There's a man upstairs, who has a puppy for you," Grandmother insisted, starting up the stairs with my sisters. She was carrying little Anne, and holding Helen by the hand as she ascended.

"She's lying," I thought again, but it was too late to stop. She and my sisters were halfway up the staircase, and I had no choice but to follow.

The door was opened by a friendly looking, young woman, who ushered us inside, and soon a big, young man made his appearance. He didn't seem to speak our language. The way he spoke sounded funny to me, though I could understand a lot of what he was saying.

The man smiled at my sisters and me and tried to be friendly but I didn't want any part of it. Grandmother was talking quietly with him, sounding nervous. There was no puppy in evidence, as I knew there wouldn't be.

The thought crossed my mind that maybe he was a doctor who would be giving us shots or doing something else that hurt. Grownups always lied about doctors, and played tricks to get you there without a fuss. I hoped they weren't going to tie me up and cut me open again like the last time at the hospital. Now I was really scared, because I sensed that something really awful was about to happen. My sisters were huddled together, very quiet.

Grandmother exchanged a few words with the young woman, then pointing to the man, turned to me: "This is Ian. He will take you to your parents. Remember always, you are the oldest, you are responsible for your younger sisters."

With that she turned and fled out the door through which we'd entered. I tried to follow, to stop her from leaving us behind, but the young woman was faster. She quickly locked the door and put the key in her pocket.

Stunned, I turned around to face my frightened, sobbing sisters. Two helpless and terrified little girls – still babies, really -- who were now my "responsibility."

Having secured us inside, the woman left the room and we were alone with the young man who seemed at a loss. My sisters were crying inconsolably. I didn't know what to do either, so I just stood there saying: "Don't cry, don't cry, we're going to see Mom and Dad." I didn't for a moment believe this, but I would say anything to make them stop crying.

Finally, Helen asked through her tears; "Where are they?"

"I don't know, but Ian does and he will take us there,"

"Really?" Helen wanted reassurance.

Something shifted inside me. Years before I'd learned to swallow my own emotions and to pretend. I was the big girl here, and big people lied about everything, especially about feelings. I pushed my own terror and anger down.

"Of course," I replied, voicing a conviction I didn't feel. "Didn't you hear what Grandmother said?" Helen's sobs became sniffles and eventually stopped. Anne followed suit. We started looking around.

Presently, the woman reappeared holding a plate of chocolates. She offered it to me first. I shook my head, no. I didn't trust her or Ian. They were strangers, possibly enemies. I wasn't going to be bribed with a chocolate. She turned to my sisters, who were showing decided interest in the offer. I sprang forward like a mother cat protecting her kittens. "Don't touch it", I shouted, "It

could be poisoned." My little sisters stared at me in confusion. The woman took a piece and ate it. She gave one to the man, who ate it too. "See, it's safe," she said handing it again to the little ones, who no longer hesitated. She offered it again to me. I felt foolish. The candy was not poisoned and had it been, I saw how little power I had to influence and keep safe the sisters, for whom I had been made responsible.

I ate a piece of the chocolate, but its sweetness tasted bitter in my mouth. The full extent of aloneness and ensuing fear hit me full force, like a punch in the gut.

Years later, I realized how abandoned I had been by Grandmother's cowardly retreat. I was powerless to fulfill the responsibility assigned by her and which became a crushing burden to a six-year old child.

At that time, I only felt scared. Scared of being left alone, scared of not being able to protect myself or the sisters left in my care, terrified of what could happen to us. And I knew that, at all cost, I had to keep these feelings to myself.

TEN

Stolen Apples

WE WERE ILLEGALLY CROSSING BORDERS IN THE COMPANY OF the young stranger, Ian, whom we called "Uncle", and each crossing threatened immediate death, if caught. In the year 1948, when we were making our escape from the Iron Curtain, Soviet border guards shot first and asked questions later, if anyone was still alive to answer them.

"Uncle" spoke Czech not Polish, but fortunately the languages were similar enough so that between the words and gestures we were able to manage essential messages: hungry, tired, thirsty, need bathroom. That was about it. I had no idea where we were going and would not have believed him anyway.

Our situation was completely fantastic and surreal. We were three very young children, travelling with a stranger who didn't speak our language to an unknown destination.

The only thing we all understood was that there was great danger. Ian told us that if the Bad Men found us, they would kill him and take us far away, so that we would never see our family again. More danger. No sense of safety or security. In fact, anything but.

I kept a blank face whenever Ian repeated this warning,

though it shook me to my bones. I knew what killing meant as I had seen many dead corpses on our exit from Warsaw after the fall of the City. Ian – "Uncle" -- was a stranger, but a benign one. He did not hurt us, and protected us from the Bad Men. He was very clear and very strict about what we had to do to stay safe: no talking, no crying and no noise of any kind. I doubt if my younger sisters had any idea of what was going on, but they were intimidated enough to be unnaturally quiet and obedient. I understood more, and was more frightened.

Often, we travelled lonely country roads by night, hiding in a ditch when the rare farm wagon rumbled by. By day, we slept in strange cottages or under trees in the woods. It was November and starting to get cold. The three of us would snuggle together for warmth and comfort. Uncle would cover us with a sort of blanket he carried, then pile dry leaves on top of us both for additional warmth and camouflage.

We had been travelling for days, mostly on foot, sometimes by train. Two weeks into this trip, we were hungry and footsore.

One clear autumnal day: cool, crisp and sunny, we were walking through an apple orchard. Anne had started crying softly. She was very hungry. We had had some stale bread for breakfast many hours ago, and now it was late afternoon and we hadn't eaten since. I felt my empty stomach rumble.

Uncle set Anne down by the side of the road and motioned us to sit next to her. He then went around picking apples left after the harvest and stuffing them in his pockets.

"You can't take these apples," I informed him. "That's stealing."

He laughed and passed us the fruit. My sisters ate hungrily. I refused the apple.

"No, it's stolen," I repeated.

He put it back in his pocket. We continued the endless hours of walking.

After some time he offered the apple again, and this time I

took it. I felt shame, but could no longer resist the pangs of hunger.

By now, I had experienced the total loss of everything familiar that had once shaped my reality. Gone were Danda and my parents and my family. Gone were my room, my toys and my home. All that was left were my sisters and I keenly felt the burden of a responsibility that I was constantly reminded I could not fulfill. I felt guilt and shame for being unable to protect them, as charged to do by Grandmother. These feelings were about to become even more acute.

Meanwhile, all I had to hold onto was my own self, a small soul that was held together by an ever more rigid commitment to the rules of the past. In the face of losing everything else, holding on to the concepts of right and wrong and allegiance to fairness and justice became acute. This hyper-vigilance and rigid commitment to issues was a life raft... for now. It held me together and gave meaning to an otherwise dark and menacing world. Rules and a sense of justice were all I had left of the world that had been torn away from me.

ELEVEN

Losing Anne

WE HAD TO CROSS FOUR BORDERS: FROM POLAND TO Czechoslovakia, from Czechoslovakia to East Germany, then the most difficult one to West Germany and finally to Belgium, where – so we were told -- our Mother was waiting.

The first two were within the Iron Curtain; the third into West Germany meant crossing out of Soviet control into the West, making it the most difficult and dangerous one. The truth was, it would have been fatal to have been caught anywhere. It's just that being apprehended on a Soviet border meant most likely instant death for us all, while if we were caught in the West it would mean deportation back to Czechoslovakia first -- with the same end result for Uncle and permanent deportation deep into the Soviet Union for us. Our parents and family would never have known what became of us.

The first border was relatively easy. Both Poland and Czechoslovakia were under Communist rule. The Carpathian Mountains formed a natural border between the two countries, and visitors including tourists and holiday-makers were not unusual. Uncle was very familiar with the terrain and the mountain passes we had to traverse. In addition, he knew 'safe houses' where we could stay the night, and had resources such as family and friends he could call on. We were relatively safe travelling through Czechoslovakia, especially since he was a native citizen and had a passport. Sometimes, we were able to catch a ride on a train for a short distance, or on a hay wagon.

East Germany became more tricky, as spies and smugglers were rampant and a Czech travelling with three Polish children, and without proper documents would have a lot of explaining to do. We had to stay out of sight not only of soldiers and police, but also civilians who might report suspicious strangers to the authorities.

So, from here the trip became progressively more dangerous as well as more taxing. Food was harder to come by, it became necessary to travel mostly at night and always by foot. Adding to our hardships, the weather was getting colder and we had only dresses and light sweaters to keep warm.

Finally, we arrived at the West German border and suddenly Uncle saw a dreadful surprise. Since his previous crossings, in addition to the barbed wire, which he expected, the Soviets had dug a deep ditch and it was filled waist high with water. It was impossible for me to cross on my own, and he could not carry all three of us at once. It must have been a terrible dilemma for him, but he was a survivor and not about to give up. He knew he had to move fast, as lingering at any border, especially this particular one, was a recipe for disaster. So he devised a plan.

He knew that as the oldest, I understood the extent of the threat more than the others, and was more terrified, so he decided he couldn't leave me alone. He wasn't sure about four-year old Helen, but knew than Anne, who was not yet three years old, understood the least and was least likely to panic if left alone. He decided to take her across to the other side, and then return for Helen and me.

We sat huddled together under a fence, a short distance from the border and hidden by some bushes. I understood what he said. We were to sit silently and wait without moving until his return. If men with guns came by, we were to sit very still so they would not find us. It was the middle of the night and the sky was black but there was a full moon throwing an eerie light on our surroundings. I was terrified.

"Did you hear that noise?" I whispered to Helen.

"No," she answered.

We sat in silence. Suddenly, I heard it again.

"Helen, I hear a noise, don't you hear it?"

"No, hush," she replied.

But now the noise was undeniable… *and it was coming toward us.*

"Helen", I cried. " I hear dogs barking. They're coming to get us."

"Shush," She repeated. "Let's pray."

We held hands and feverishly repeated over and over:

Angel of God, our guardian dear…

And: *Hail Mary, full of grace…Holy Mary, Mother of God pray for us sinners now and in the hour of our death….*

We didn't want Her to pray for us in the hour of our death, but rather to save us from that scary fate. But those were the only prayers we knew that answered most closely our immediate need.

Still, the dogs kept barking, their terrible sound coming closer. We repeated the prayers over and over for a long time. Unexpectedly, the barking stopped.

We sat quietly in silent terror. And then we heard cautious steps approaching. My heart was in my throat and Helen was squeezing me with all her might. With great relief, we recognized the figure of Uncle in the darkness.

He picked us both up and carried us to the ditch, leaving me on one side while taking Helen across. I could see her sitting on the other side while he came to get me. When we were all safely on the other side and we started walking.

"Where's Anne?" I asked.

"Don't talk", he whispered, "She's not far."

We continued walking until we came to a small clearing. Two paths diverged beyond. I could feel Uncle's sudden tension. He ran ahead peeking under bushes.

"She's gone", He whispered urgently. "This is where I left her. I told her not to move but she did. I have to check the path to the left. You two stay here and don't go anywhere."

Obediently, we sat down. I was devastated. I wasn't supposed to let this happen. I let my sister get lost.

Soon, Uncle returned, alone.

"I can't find her, but we can't stay here. It's not safe. We must move on."

"You lost Anne," I whispered angrily. "We can't just go on. You have to find her first."

He scooped Helen in his arms. "It's too dangerous to stay here longer. We'll all get killed. Stay if you like. We're leaving."

I watched them disappear in the trees.

It was a terrible moment. I was trying to do everything right, fulfill my responsibilities. Yet, no matter how hard I tried I was doomed to fail. I could not force Uncle to do the right thing, to find Anne or die trying. Once again I had no power.

Something broke inside and panic seized me. I knew it was wrong to abandon my little sister who was my responsibility, but I was too scared, not brave enough to do the right thing. Just like I gave in to my hunger and ate the stolen apples, I now gave in to fear and ran after them. I was becoming someone I didn't like very much, but I was also becoming numb to feelings, starting not to care anymore.

They were not far ahead and I caught up quickly. At least Uncle did not humiliate me with a lecture, and we walked silently for almost an hour. Suddenly, we heard the sound of rustling leaves up ahead. Quickly, Uncle hid us in the under-brush, and stealthily crept forward to investigate.

A few minutes later, he came running back with Anne in

his arms. Miraculously, she chose the right path and stayed on it. It had been a close call.

Overburdening a child with a task she can never possibly do right crushes the spirit. My already well-developed judgment turned inward and I started to blame myself. Over and over I had failed to do what was right.

I was starting to see myself in a negative light. Since nothing seemed to make sense anymore, life was not following the rules I had grown up with and I had no power to make things right, I began not to care. I started to become numbed to feelings as they all were painful. What I didn't realize then, was that numbness, while protecting from pain would also dull positive feelings of happiness and joy.

TWELVE

Arriving in Belgium

IT SEEMED LIKE MONTHS SINCE GRANDMOTHER HAD abandoned us in the apartment with Ian. The journey felt endless, though in fact we were only three weeks on the road. I was hungry and cold, but mostly so very tired.

I was tired of being constantly terrified that we'd be caught. And on a very simple, human level my feet and legs ached. It didn't seem fair that Uncle always carried Anne and sometimes Helen but never me. I knew that was because I was the oldest, but it still didn't seem fair.

After we crossed that most difficult and dangerous border into West Germany, for sure, life became marginally easier. Three years after the end of War, Europe was still full of war refugees and displaced persons trying to find their way home, or trying to find a new home. Uncle spoke German, and that made it easier for him to blend in. Travelling with three very young children who only spoke Polish, however, presented a hazard. We had to continue to stay under the radar.

When we crossed the final boundary into Belgium, Uncle was palpably relieved. His face brightened and his step quickened. We were on safer turf, further away from the Soviet block, and finally on the home stretch of our journey.

Although my sisters and I had no understanding of the reasons, we were able to sense the lessening of tension. Food became more plentiful. But the long hard trip had taken its toll.

We were all nearing exhaustion. The hunger, cold, lack of sound sleep and constant fear had repressed and drained our normal energy and vivacity. We had become quiet, restrained, obedient children – ghosts of our former selves – bearing no resemblance to the boisterous little girls we had been before. Though amazingly, we still had the same bows in our hair we had been wearing at the start of the journey.

Though I didn't talk about it, I had never believed that we were being taken to our parents. The fact was, they were no longer very real to me. Nor, was I longing to go back to my toys and the safety of home and family. Somehow, that memory too became distant and unreal. All I wanted was for the travel to end. I wanted a warm bed to sleep in, and lots of food to eat, whenever I was hungry. And, most of all, I didn't want to walk anymore. I just wanted to rest and for someone to carry me. I wanted to feel safe. I felt more empty than I had ever felt in my young life. Dead in a way.

In retrospect, I also wanted to lay down the heavy burden of responsibility for my sisters. I needed an adult, any adult, to take responsibility for *me*. I wanted someone to parent *me*, take care of a not yet six-year old, still a child but in many respects forced to carry the burdens of an adult.

We had been constantly promised that Brussels would be the end of the endless journey, and this hope motivated me to go on. Brussels became a symbol of safety, food, rest and a warm bed. Finally, it seemed that my hopes and dreams were about to come true. We arrived at the gates of beautiful, shining Brussels, where Mom was awaiting us, along with warm beds and lots of food. It was late evening and the broad, tree-lined avenue was bordered by large, round stone boulders. A bright moon cast a white glow on the surroundings.

Tall street lamps illuminated the way. Everything was so clean and orderly, so beautiful, it looked and felt magical. I knew this was the end of our journey.

It was night and the gates to the City were closed. At each side there stood a soldier in uniform holding a rifle. Our ragged group approached and Uncle, putting Anne down, stepped forward. He addressed the soldiers.

"Passports." The soldier was curt.

Uncle pulled some papers out of his pocket and handed them to the Guard. The soldier looked them over, and asked some questions. He handed the papers to his colleague, who shook his head, and thrust them back at Uncle.

"False," He said, "You cannot enter."

Although they spoke a foreign language, I understood perfectly what was being said. I understood that the soldiers wouldn't let us in, that there won't be warm beds or food or an end to the misery of the past weeks. We would now have to make the whole arduous trip in reverse.

They spoke back and forth for some time, and Uncle tried to argue pointing at us. It was useless and I had never seen him look so defeated, so hopeless. He looked as tired as I felt.

As he picked up Anne and started walking away, motioning us to follow, something snapped inside me. I was done. I sat on the nearest boulder and refused to move. Uncle kept calling me and walking away, carrying little Anne and holding Helen by the hand, believing I would follow. But I could not. I didn't care anymore about being abandoned or killed. I was completely numb even to fear, and didn't care about anything: I wasn't going back. I couldn't do it anymore. I was just too tired.

The guards looked at me and at each other. After what seemed an eternity, they nodded their heads and called Uncle back. They opened the gates and waved us through.

As the vision of food and a warm bed again became a reality in my benumbed brain, I felt a sudden surge of energy, jumped off my perch on the boulder and followed Uncle and my sisters into the city. After having travelled for weeks through nothing but war-ravaged towns, and off the beaten path, backwoods villages, Brussels seemed like a place out of a fairy tale. Wide avenues were illuminated by tall street lamps. There were no bedraggled people milling about. Everything looked safe and inviting.

"How much farther do we have to go?" I asked tugging at his sleeve.

He pointed to a bus stopped at the corner.

"We're going to ride."

"Is it safe? Aren't they going to catch us?" I was eager at the thought of riding instead of walking, but still very anxious.

"No, we're safe now," he smiled.

We got on the bus and I looked around curiously. People speaking a language I didn't understand were what we had encountered throughout the entire trip, so that was nothing new. It was a relief that they seemed busy with their own conversations paying no attention to us. Perhaps this bus was indeed safe. I had not been convinced by Uncle's assurances. After all, I knew from past experience that adults lied a lot and could not be trusted. Best to be on the lookout. To my relief, no one seemed to pay us any attention.

Something had changed in me during our journey. Safety and survival had become my goals.

The bus ride took a long time, and my exhausted sisters fell asleep, but I did not. I needed to be on the lookout for danger, and notice as best as I could where we were going. I was still on guard and ready for a quick escape.

The bus stopped in front of a nice looking hotel. There were more trees around the entrance and a doorman in uniform stood in front of the bronze door.

"I hope he lets us in", I thought. This looked like a good place to stay and visions of food and a warm bed again infused my tired brain. Uncle spoke to the doorman and showed him the papers. For a moment I almost panicked. These were the same papers the soldiers didn't like. I wondered why he didn't show the doorman different ones. But my fears were unfounded and the door opened wide for us to enter.

We walked like in a dream through across the ornate, marble lobby and under the heavy brass chandeliers up to the desk.

"You can relax in these chairs while I talk to the lady, who will get your room ready."

What room? I just wanted to eat and sleep but knew I would have to wait for the answers to reveal themselves. But I also felt tense. We piled all three into one of the large uphol-stered chairs, finding warmth and comfort in huddling together. Although the room was warm enough, our bodies still remembered the pervasive cold and damp of the long days and nights spent outdoors, and we craved all the heat we could get.

It didn't take long. Soon, Uncle took us to a dining room, empty at this time of night, and we were seated at a table. Little Anne was fidgety and I held her on my lap in the spacious, comfortable chair. To my delight, hot soup and warm bread with butter were served. We were in heaven. Warm and with full bellies we were having trouble keeping our eyes open.

Uncle was talking and I tried hard to take it all in. He told us the Mom was not here, had to leave and was waiting with Dad for us in a place called America. The fact that Mom was not here was not news. I never believed that fable.

"I'm not walking anymore," I said. "I like this place. I want to stay here."

He laughed. "You won't have to walk to America."

"Can we go to sleep now?" I asked as my sisters were again nodding off and I had the greatest difficulty staying awake myself.

I didn't really care about America, in fact, I was well past caring. I hadn't expected Mom to be in Belgium, and I didn't expect her to be someplace called America. We had been told so many times that we were going to see them, and we never did. That hope stopped being a part of my reality. It was no longer what I was striving for. All I wanted was a warm place with lots of food that was safe from bad people who wanted to hurt us. This hotel felt like it was such a place and for now I was content. I just wanted to sleep.

A young girl in a uniform appeared at our table. She smiled and reached for sleeping Anne.

"She'll take you to your room now, and you can sleep as long as you like." He said. Unexpectedly, he planted a kiss on Anne's head, then hugged Helen and me.

"It's time to say goodbye."

"Where are you going to sleep?" I asked disturbed by the seriousness of his words.

"I have to go back," he replied.

Now I understood. He too was going to abandon us -- like my beloved Danda, and our parents and our Grandmother. He was about to leave us alone to face the unknown and leave me alone with the responsibility for my sisters.

"No," I cried out grabbing a hold of his jacket. "No, don't go."

"I must go. But you are safe now, and you will be all right. Soon you will go to America and be with your Mom and Dad. Your mother's friend will be here tomorrow to take care of you. You will be all right, trust me."

He stooped down to kiss me and disengage his jacket from my tightly clenched hand. Then he quickly walked away.

I did not believe him, but I had no power to stop him. I understood that further resistance was futile. Despite my fear of being left alone with my sisters, once again at the mercy of strangers, I knew I had no power to make him stay. Without a word, I followed the girl to an elevator.

We ascended a few floors, then walked down a corridor, our feet sinking into the plush carpet. She opened a door and I saw a big bed with crisp white sheets and warm covers. I stood transfixed, while the girl undressed us and we piled in. Warmth enveloped us and I went off into a long, dreamless sleep.

Many hours later, I woke feeling Helen and Anne stirring. The sun was shining brightly through the long windows. I had not felted this rested in a long time, but now I was very hungry. Anne demanded breakfast and Helen agreed. We were all ready to eat!

There was a little problem. We were all naked like the day we were born, and I vaguely remembered the night before how the girl in uniform had removed our clothes, which had no been washed for three long weeks, before tucking us into bed. The clothes were nowhere in sight. We'll have to find someone, I decided.

And so, we walked out, down the plush carpeted hall and to the elevator. I knew the way as I had carefully memorized it the night before. The elevator was the European style: an open grill without a solid door. I didn't know how to get it to work it. I decided to wait for someone going up or down and ask for help.

Soon, there was the sound of the lift door opening and closing on a floor above. The whirring sound announced it was in action. When it reached our landing I called out – "Help!" -- in Polish. In the lift, stood a very stiff, very erect gentleman carrying a cane, and formally dressed in a suit, coat, scarf and hat.

A look of astonishment and consternation crossed his face. Seeing three naked little girls, his eyes went wide. He mumbled something and continued his descent.

In response to the news that three naked children were at large on the fourth floor, the maid came hurrying with our clothes. We got dressed and finally got our breakfast. Life was getting better.

Late that evening, Mother's friend arrived from Paris. She spoke Polish and explained she would take care of us until we could go to our parents. I discounted the latter part, but was pleased that our new caretaker could communicate with us in Polish. When she assured me that we didn't have to travel anywhere and would be staying at this safe hotel with a warm bed and lots of food, I was satisfied. I didn't believe it would last, but for the present life was definitely improved.

Life at the hotel was so good compared to the privations we had suffered on our journey, that for a while I had no complaints. But as days turned into weeks, it started to feel like we would be staying there forever. It started feeling more like an ornate, luxurious prison. The warm bed and plentiful food were no longer enough. I longed for the first time for a home, like the home I had had and lost. I missed my toys, the house the garden, and the large extended family. I missed my cousin Andy, who frequently came to play. When I asked 'Auntie' when we would go home, she would explain that we were going to a new home, to our parents in America.

But I didn't want a new home. I didn't want to go to "America," whatever that was. I wanted to go home. By this time I had learned. Keep everything to yourself. It's dangerous to cry. Only a picture of Christmas in Brussels reveals the reality of our feelings. It shows the faces of three sad, frightened little girls. One of them was like a coiled spring, waiting for the worst to happen.

And so I was depleted of emotional resources. Unable to trust that any adult would really be there for me, I knew I was on my own. But I had also, by now, come to realize my inability to control events, people or even my own actions. The feelings of fear were overpowering. So was the feeling of failure, because I was powerless to choose the right action when overwhelmed by circumstances.

I knew that whatever was going to happen now would be completely out of my control. I was like a cornered animal just trying to anticipate and avoid danger, just trying to survive, or like a prisoner trying to avoid more torture at any cost.

A wary hyper-vigilance had set in.

THIRTEEN

End of Journey

DESPITE APPEARANCES, MY PARENTS DID NOT INTEND TO LEAD us on a wild goose chase. When advised in Switzerland that they could not return to Poland, they immediately started inquiries as to how they could get us out. Unbeknownst to the authorities, Dad had left Poland with three hundred thousand American dollars, a third belonging to him and two thirds to his two sisters. In 1939, suspecting that the bulk of his fortune might be lost in the war, my Grandfather had given each of his five children one hundred thousand American dollars. When Dad was leaving the country, two of his sisters requested he take their share along with his for safe-keeping, perhaps in a foreign bank. So, he had cash.

They found a professional smuggler, who had successfully escorted people out of the Iron Curtain countries and hired him to smuggle us, and Grandmother out of Poland. My parents were to wait in Brussels, at the agreed hotel for further communication from him.

Immediately however they ran into problems. For some reason, Dad was unable to get a Belgian visa, so it was decided he would fly to New York City and Mom would go to Brussels to wait for us. This they did, and she waited and waited to hear that we were on our way. After several weeks of silence, she got a phone call from the smuggler requesting she obtain false passports for us. Mother was stunned and horrified. She was staying in a foreign country, had absolutely no contacts, and no idea how to go about getting false papers. After explaining this, she reminded him that the ten thousand dollars he had demanded and received was meant to pay for all the expenses of getting us out. He said he would try.

Then came the second, third and fourth calls. He insisted that without false papers he could not get us out. Mother became worried that these calls could get her in trouble. This was the time before automatic, direct connections, and every call had to go through an operator, who could listen in at will. She told him to stop calling, and that was the last she heard from him. The money was gone, and they were back to square one.

I don't know how they found "Uncle." He was a young student at the University of Prague, who had been smuggling people out of Communist countries to the West. After the war and about to be married, he needed money, and this trip was to be his last one. His fiancée wanted him out of the dangerous business. Despite Mother's pleas, he absolutely refused to take Grandmother. He felt that he could not safely handle three little girls and an elderly lady. He was hired, and Mother began again to hope and wait.

Unfortunately, she was correct in fearing trouble as a result of the earlier calls.

One of the hotel phone operators was Polish and did listen in. She reported the talk about false passports and papers to the police. Suspected of being a spy, Mother was called in for questioning. She told the truth and the authorities must have found her believable as she was not detained. Nevertheless, when her three-month visitor visa came up for renewal she was refused and had to leave the country. She had a visa for the United States and had no choice but to join Dad in New York.

Before she left, she made arrangements with the hotel to call a Polish friend in Paris immediately upon our arrival. The friend had agreed, should we ever arrive, to come immediately to Brussels and care for us at the hotel, until we could fly to join our parents in the States.

Although Mom had received a secret signal from the family that we had left Poland, there could be no further news or communication until we arrived in Brussels. There was no way of knowing when, or even if, we would make it out safely. There was nothing they could do but pray, hope and wait for news.

Furthermore, we still didn't have any legal passports or papers. The border guards recognized the false ones 'Uncle' had for us and it was impossible for us to get into the States with them. It took my parents weeks to creatively solve that particular difficulty, and it was two months before we were finally put on a plane to New York.

At the end of January of 1949, the fateful evening arrived. We were bundled to the airport and loaded on a plane. Auntie kissed us good-bye, telling us again that we were going to our parents. A nice lady, who spoke a few words of Polish, would take us to them. She turned out to be the stewardess (now flight attendant). I wondered where we were really going.

I had never been on a plane before. The couple across the aisle spoke Polish and took us under their wing. The Lady seemed very nice, she answered my questions about food and the loo. These were the matters of immediate importance. Once the Stewardess brought us snacks to munch on, I knew that we would not go hungry. The cabin was warm and the seats comfortable. I relaxed and waited to see what would happen next.

The plane took off. After some time, the Stewardess brought us dinner. Our bellies full, we settled down to sleep.

We woke in the gray light of the morning, and the Stewardess brought our breakfast. The lady across the aisle told me it wouldn't be long now. We would be landing in New York soon.

I started wondering if perhaps what we had been told so many times was true after all. Were we really going to our parents? Until now, I had dismissed this possibility as a lie, but now I was wondering. Could it be true? Would they take us back home? I pictured them in my mind, and suddenly, for the first time in many months I hoped it was true. I wanted to see them again.

The plane was going around in big circles, and I asked the nice Lady when we would be landing. She explained that there was a problem. Apparently, there was a lot of fog on the ground and many planes had to wait in line before they were allowed to land. We, too, had to wait our turn. It could take a while, and it did.

After an hour or so of circling above Idlewild (now Kennedy) airport, an announcement came on the cabin loud-speaker. The Lady translated for me. Because of the fog and big backup of planes waiting to land in New York, our pilot decided we had to go to Boston instead. She reassured me that we would all be put on a train to New York, and that we would find our parents there. I didn't really care. This was just a continuation of our unwelcome travel adventures but at least it did not feel dangerous like the earlier part. We were fed when hungry, had a warm place to sleep, and, most impor-tantly, I didn't have to walk for days.

We landed in Boston, and were put on a train. The nice couple and the nice stewardess came with us. This was comforting, as I felt cared for and safe. Again, we had food and it was warm. I had learned to go with the flow, even if I had no idea where it was taking us.

In the end, we got to New York and were taken to two people who excitedly advanced toward us. I was holding both my sisters by the hand, and stepped back. I took a careful look at them and for a moment wasn't sure. Then Mom called my name. I looked again and knew it was them. Helen was unconvinced.

"Are you sure?" she asked.

"Yes," I replied. "I recognize Mom's brown silk blouse."

"What about Dad?" she continued, uncertainty in her voice.

"It's him. He has the hole in his hand." Indeed, as a result of a war wound, Dad's hand was deformed in a particular way, and I recognized him by that mark.

She agreed, and we stepped closer allowing a tentative embrace. When Mom tried to take Anne's hand, however, she started screaming. I quickly grabbed her and placed her between Helen and me. Anne had been only about a year old when she last saw our parents and to her they were complete strangers. Helen and I recognized that they were our parents, but it would take a very long time for us to relate to them as such. Whatever our feelings, this was the beginning of a completely new chapter in our young lives.

It seemed on the surface like a happy ending. Three little children re-united with their parents, poised to enjoy a new life in a new country in the security of a new home –safe and happy at last. But there was a lot of old baggage unrecognized and unresolved on the inside.

I had nightmares and severe anxiety. I was afraid of the dark and of being alone. The seeds of insecurity and mistrust had been sown… deeply. They would continue to sprout and cause damage.

And as if the burdens of the past were not enough, I was about to be tasked with yet another impossible mission. For me, the nightmare was not yet over, and would not be over for a long, long time.

Living in Darkness

All war survivors are left with the effects and scars of trauma. I was only seven years old, young and resilient enough for the healing to begin under new and auspicious circumstances. Unfortunately, the circumstances in which we found ourselves were not conducive to healing. My sisters and I were not the only survivors carrying the trauma.

I was very young when Dad gave me a book to read: "*Kamienie na Szaniec*". It was written by a Warsaw freedom fighter with vivid descriptions of the atrocities committed by the Nazis against the Polish Underground during the years of occupation. I learned for the first time about male testicles and how, they were crushed by Gestapo boots. I read about fingernails being pulled out and a host of other vivid and unimaginable tortures. There were names and drawings. Dad pointed out the young men he had known personally, his dead friends. I was profoundly traumatized, yet could not stop reading. I had to know.

My parents and all the adults I would grow up with had suffered much more than I had. They had lost family, friends, home and country under horrific circumstances. Their lives were ravaged, first by war then by the Soviet occupation. They had not come to America by choice, looking for a better life. They came of necessity, to survive and endure until Poland was free of the Communist yoke and they could return to rebuild their country and their lives. They never considered themselves permanent residents but rather temporary guests in a country, which provided them with a safe haven. The intention was to go back home.

FOURTEEN

Little Poland

IT COULD BE SAID THAT WE GREW UP IN "LITTLE POLAND," AS the atmosphere, customs and ideas had nothing to do with the country in which we resided. I was isolated from local peers and had no friends or companions except for my sisters. We went to an excellent private school, as education was a high priority for my Dad. Every morning, he drove us there. He didn't want of us going on the bus. After classes were over, there was lunch and a study hall followed by sports. This was the time when friendships were made and one socialized with peers. After the first few weeks, Dad decided this was not necessary, so he picked us up right after classes every day.

"Dad, why can't we go on the bus with our friends?" I asked. "I really want to stay for lunch at school. It's fun. And when you pick us up right after classes, we never get to play the games in the afternoon. The other kids think we're strange."

"You're not strange. You're different. And you are supposed to be different. You are special. Did you forget your are Poles not Americans?"

"No, Dad." I whispered ashamed that a part of me wanted to be like the others.

"Good," he would say cheerfully closing the subject. "Let's hear no more about it."

We lived on forty acres, just outside a four-hundred acre fruit orchard owned by Father, and the only children within walking distance were those of farm workers. We were not allowed to play with them. We never had bikes or learned to ride because for some reason Dad considered it unladylike. During the school year, we played with each other, and during the summer there were Polish kids attending the summer scout camps sponsored by my parents. As time went by, the life of my sisters became somewhat less restricted, but as the oldest, I never had any American friends.

Adults who visited or lived with us for extended periods, were all Polish emigres, like us, waiting to return home Many of our guests were concentration camp survivors. Others, arriving from the displaced person camps in Europe, where they had been housed after the war, had trouble finding jobs at first, and would live with us for weeks or months. They were all disoriented and traumatized by their experiences and losses, and by the uncertain future they faced in a foreign land.

Once, an elderly lady came to visit. The day was hot and she took off her cardigan. A set of pale blue numbers tattooed on her forearm caught my immediate attention. I was mystified never having seen such a thing before, and curiosity overcame my shyness.

"What are those blue numbers for?" I asked innocently. The woman became flustered and quickly covered her arm.

"It's nothing, just something from the past," She mumbled.

Now I was embarrassed sensing that I had intruded on something private and painful. Mom apologized and pulled me away. She said it was never right to ask people about such marks because it was too painful for people to talk about it. Later, I asked Mom about the mystery. She explained that the Nazis imprisoned people in concentration camps during the war, and tattooed numbers on their arms. It was a very sad and dreadful time so people don't want to talk about it. I should never bring it up again.

"But why did they do it?" I persisted. "Didn't it hurt?"

"Of course, but it hurt a lot less than all the other things the Nazis did to them."

"Like what?" I wanted to know.

"Like beat, torture, starve and kill them in horrible ways," Mom replied.

I sensed the sadness in her and stopped asking. I wanted and at the same time was afraid, to find out more. In a strange way, I started to identify with the victim's suffering. Inside of me, I felt vividly the fear and pain I knew they had suffered. It was unbearable, so I turned away and tried not to think about it, but my frequent nightmares would not let me forget.

Occasionally, a family or couple needed a place for a few nights, and my sister and I had give up our room and sleep on the living room floor. I resented this and felt selfish for feeling that way. Perhaps, if it had been explained to me, or if I had been given some voice in the matter, I would have felt differently. But it was just assumed that giving a homeless person a place to sleep was the right thing to do, and that there was no need to discuss it. The imposition probably activated my earlier feelings of powerlessness. I did not feel giving and generous. I felt resentful and guilty.

"Mr. and Mrs. Gorski will be staying tonight. You girls will have to give up your room and sleep on the mattresses in the living room," Mom would announce.

"Why do we always have to give up our room? It's not fair," I would complain.

"That is the most selfish thing I have heard from you in some time. I'm very disappointed. Those poor people have suffered tremendously and you whine about giving them your room for the night? I thought better of you." Mom was shocked and hurt at the lack of generosity exhibited by me. I had let her down again, as usual.

At home, we were expected to behave like ladies. There was no shouting or loud displays of emotion. Laughter was tolerated if not too noisy, but no crying or angry words, no hysterical outbursts of any kind, and certainly no tantrums. Self-control was a sign of good manners and good character. It was expected and required. Although Mom finally convinced Dad to allow us to wear long pants when playing outside, and even shorts in the heat of summer, he never liked it. And, it was unthinkable to come to the table for a meal without a skirt or dress on. At the table, children did not speak unless spoken to, and any breach of manners provoked a serious rebuke.

"Dad, what's wrong with wearing pants? Everybody does it."

"You are not everybody. You are well born, Polish young ladies and will behave as such." Another dead end.

FIFTEEN

Cut off from the World

IT WAS IMPORTANT FOR MY PARENTS TO MAKE SURE MY SISTERS and I grew up closely identified with our national heritage, and did not to succumb to the temptation of becoming in any way Americanized. To this end, we were isolated as much as possible from our peers. We were transported to school and back by our Father, and did not participate in sports or social events at school. We had no television, did not listen to the radio and did not have English books available to read at home. So, we were completely disconnected not only from contact with other kids, but also from the current culture. This made me very different from my classmates. Also, whether from innate shyness or from a sense of not belonging, I tended to be a loner and did not actively pursue friendships.

However, I did feel lonely, and when one of my classmates invited me to join the Brownies, I was excited. It would give me a chance to make some friends, to do fun things.

"Mom," I shouted when we got home. "Can I join Brownies?"

"I don't think so", she replied. "You are a Polish Girl Scout".

That was true, of course. We had been signed-up as soon

as we were eligible. Mom was a Girl Guide, a Troop leader in Warsaw, and my parents were keen to promote Polish scouting in America as a means of training and educating Polish youth in their mission as Polish patriots. We needed to be knowledgeable about our country, tough, disciplined with good survival skills in case we had to fight, and totally dedicated to the cause. Polish scouting was a perfect crucible for honing these skills.

I had become a Polish Girl Scout and went to my first camp at age nine. It was a great adventure, and at first it was fun. I felt at home among my peers. I was not different. I was not a foreigner. I was not the 'Other'. We all spoke the same language, sang the same songs and were raised on the same stories. We held the same values and had the same hopes and dreams for a liberated Poland and our place in its future.

But I wanted to try something new and different, meet other children.

"Why not, Mom? Why can't I be both? It sounds like fun and Polish Girl Scout camps are only in the summer. American Brownies meet all year. I can make friends."

"But you are *not* an American. You are a *Pole*. Your Dad and I would be very disappointed if you ever forgot that."

"I will never forget, Mom. This is just for fun. Please, please let me."

The answer was, no. When I asked Dad why not, I heard the usual response:

"Because I said so." There was nothing more to say.

And so it was made very clear. My parents had one great overarching mission that gave purpose to their lives: They wanted to make sure what happened to Poland and its people, especially those who died, would never be forgotten. It was a sacred duty to remember.

This also meant one thing for us, their children: We would be raised as good Polish patriots, who would return to rebuild the country. Above all, our parents resisted and taught us to resist any temptation to lose or give up our Polish identity by becoming Americans.

I got this message so well that, when my parents for practical reasons decided to become naturalized citizens, I was horrified and refused. My parents explained we would still retain our Polish citizenship, but to me it felt like a betrayal. My angry, young face on the naturalization papers showed how upset it made me. Confused by my parents' action, I was determined to remain a Pole and *not* become an American.

So it was that everything in our young lives – everything -- was geared around educating us about our home country. Only the Polish language was allowed at home, and the books we read for pleasure were all in Polish. Polish was and would remain our primary language. In addition to the rich and extensive Polish literature, we read Jack London, Kipling and other English authors in Polish translation. The only books permitted in English were school textbooks. During vacations, we had tutors who taught us Polish history and geography.

This all-encompassing education – one might call it indoctrination – was not only intense, it was constant.

"I get good grades, why do we have to have summer school?" I would complain. "Other kids get the summer off. They just play. Why can't we?"

"Because you are not American kids. You are different. You have a responsibility to learn all about your country. Remember, one day you are going back and you will have a big job to do. You must be prepared."

I don't want to be different, I thought. That's why I don't have friends. I am different from all the other kids in school. None of the girls even want to be friends. We don't read the same books or have the same interests.

SIXTEEN

Sacred Duty

BEING A POLE IMPLIED BEING A ROMAN CATHOLIC. POLAND had been a Catholic country for a thousand years, since King Mieszko I was baptized and officially converted his subjects to Christianity in the year 966. Although throughout most of its long history, it was far more tolerant by law of other religions than other countries in Europe, (the famous anti-semitism and persecution of Jews did not start until the last two hundred years, after Poland repeatedly lost its sovereignty at the hands of its Germanic and Russian neighbors), there was no constitutional separation of church and state as there is in this country. Mary was officially crowned as Queen of Poland, and the Poles prided themselves on their religion. Despite many religious minorities, Polish and Catholic were synonymous.

So there was no question: We went to Church *every* Sunday, and observed *all* the Church holidays and fast-days. This was serious business, when I was growing up. It didn't matter what condition you were in. I frequently felt faint during Mass in a full church, which was hot, unventilated and had no air conditioning. In order to go to Communion, one had to fast from the night before, so an empty stomach and low blood sugar did not help. I could read a translation of the priest's Latin prayers on the Polish side of my missal and that helped a bit with the boredom and the nausea. Dad was a stickler for decorum, and my discomfort was prolonged by his insistence we be there at least ten minutes before the start.

"Better half an hour early than one minute late," he would proclaim.

When I grew older and started questioning some of the Church dogma or rules, he would remind me that, like the family, the Church was not a democracy. We were to obey and not question.

But I did question. I was a "troublesome" child, who questioned rules and argued when I thought they were unfair or wrong. This brought a harsh disciplinary response from Dad. Nevertheless in the end, I did adopt the attitudes and values of my parents. I accepted and proudly espoused the identity they had forged for me. From the time I was a very little girl, I knew that I was a Pole and a Catholic. It was definitely the very best thing one could be, and being IT made me very special. Or, perhaps, because I. and my family were so special it was inevitable that we should belong to the only True religion, and be members of the finest, noblest nation.

I did not ponder these matters at the time. And if my heritage did make me feel superior to those around me -- mostly protestant Americans, as there were no blacks or Jews in my childhood experience -- the sense of superiority was one of 'noblesse oblige'. I recognized that I did not become who I was due to my own efforts, thus it was not an earned honor, rather a gift.

What became clear, however, was that this *gift* came with strings attached. As my Father was fond of saying: "Those who have been given the most, must give back the most." So I understood and accepted that having received special gifts, it was my duty in life to give back to others. This seemed only natural and right. It gave my life a definite purpose from the start. I had no idea I how would be doing this, but the concept of service to others was a given.

My parents, whose feelings I mirrored, were of course, a principal influence. For them, these matters were simple and not debatable. In the world of senseless violence and chaos into which they had been plunged during the war, and from which they emerged scarred for life, there were some certainties one had to cling to in order to preserve one's sanity and very existence. Faith in God and Country were those immutable factors, which gave life meaning, and to them, the will to go on.

With all this emphasis, training, and focus on our national religion, it made total sense to me that Catholicism was the one true faith. It was the only one established by our Lord, Himself, and all the other heresies and protestant sects were clearly created later by men. Every Sunday in church I recited in Latin -- which I understood due to the Polish translation on the other side of my missal -- the Creed: "I believe in the One, Holy, Apostolic, Catholic Church created by God." That seemed pretty clear.

And so I came to feel sorry for all my misguided neighbors who might not get to heaven due to their errors. And with my inbred sense of duty, I sincerely hoped that I would lead a life of shining example, which might influence some of them to see the light and convert.

It was, after all, my responsibility. Just as everything had always been my responsibility. I was to set a sterling example to all those around me, not only as a Catholic, but even more so as a Pole. I was a representative of Poland in a land ignorant of its history, customs and people. It was my responsibility, my sacred duty, to represent my country well.

"Whatever you do in life, good or bad will reflect on your country," Dad would say. This was a burden I carried.

What made the burden especially painful was this fact: I

was aware that my life was anything *but* a shining example. I tried hard to be perfect and was ashamed of the failures.

My sister, Helen, was a painful reminder of what I should be, but wasn't. Always understanding, patient, helpful and generous to a fault, Mom set her to me as an example. Her goodness was genuine, not put on for show. Helen was real.

"Mom, is there anything more I can do to help?' She would inquire after finishing all her chores.

"No, Dear, you've done your share. It's Ewa's turn now."

"I don't mind, Mom. Really. Ewa is reading. Let her."

Later, Mom would say to me: "Why can't you be helpful like your sister?"

I could never resent Helen. She gave me so much. Although more than a year younger, she was my alter mother, my protector. She was never afraid, or at least never admitted to it.

Helen was the one I could turn to, in the midst of all this demand and pressure, for some bit of comfort. Because, despite the solid sense of steadfastness and security on which my young life was now built, something inside was always unsteady and anxious. It was a feeling I could never quite shake, and it often erupted into my dreams.

We used to share a bedroom, and when I woke in the middle of the night in a state of terror from one of my recurring nightmares, I would whisper urgently:

"Helen, Helen, are you awake?"

"I am, now," was her sleepy reply.

"I'm scared," I whimpered, "I had a bad dream."

"Dreams aren't real. Nothing to be scared of. Go back to sleep," she would insist.

"OK, but stay awake until I do, or I'll be scared again."

"I will, but hurry up and go to sleep. I'm tired."

After a few minutes, I checked again: "Helen?"

"I'm *awake*," she would answer with some impatience. "But if you don't hurry up, I'll go to sleep."

I knew it was time to stop testing her patience, and went back to sleep. I don't know how I would have survived my childhood without Helen.

The word 'country' in Polish, like the Latin 'patria' does not mean someplace away from the city. Nor is it interchangeable with the word 'nation.' It has only one meaning: the nation-state, the Fatherland to which you belong for ethnic/historical reasons, and to which your heart and soul are inextricably linked. It is not a political belonging. It is a belonging that you do not choose and cannot escape. The worst possible failure in life would be to bring shame on my country. The greatest accomplishment and source of pride would be to bring it glory.

These beliefs were truly and deeply held. In retrospect, they would lead me to alienation, isolation and eventually to despair.

SEVENTEEN

Family Trauma

WHAT I COULD NOT HAVE KNOWN GROWING UP WAS THAT I had been severely traumatized as a little girl in Nazi-occupied Poland… and now, in America, I was being re-traumatized by an ideology that was being imposed on me and which I espoused as my own. Life was a struggle between the drive to hold on to the past and the drive to heal.

Everyone coming out of the nightmare that was Poland during the war was also traumatized by the horrors they had lived. And my early growing years in America were heavily marked, not just by our lifestyle, but also by the character and personalities of my parents, who too had been marked and deeply shaken by war-time atrocities.

My mother was born after the death of her own father, and then raised by a very young, very narcissistic mother. Grandmother did not particularly like or enjoy children and saw her own daughter as an unwelcome testimonial to her age, as well as an encumbrance and obstacle to her future remarriage and social success. She got rid of my mother by sending her to a boarding school at age six. The school was located in Warsaw where my grandmother lived, and my Mom could easily have been a day student as all the other city residents were. It must have been painfully clear to her that she was not wanted at home. I doubt if there ever was any significant mother-daughter bonding. I always thought of my mother as an orphan who, lacking both a role model and later an opportunity to care for her newborn daughter, never developed any real mothering skills.

In school, she was well liked and respected. Although not possessed of strong leadership qualities, her integrity, responsibility and devotion to duty, got her promoted to leader of the school Girl Scouting Troop. During the Nazi occupation, she was criticized for not aggressively leading the girls under her command into the ranks of the underground movement. Mother never spoke about this episode, but many years after she died her close friend explained to me the reason for this omission. During the occupation Mother acted as courier for the Polish underground repeatedly risking her life in the service of her country. Although deeply involved in the perilous work, she did not feel it right to pressure the young girls in her troop into activities, which would endanger them. She served as a glowing example of service to duty and patriotism, but left the choice of following this dangerous path to each individual girl.

She was an intelligent young woman, who distinguished herself by earning a master's degree in economics from Warsaw University, at a time when women rarely entered such fields.

When we settled in the U.S., she ran the business side of my father's fruit orchard. Competent and adaptable, she managed a household, took care of a chronically ill, very demanding and needy husband, and raised 4 daughters including at times nieces and nephews, despite the fact that she had no training or experience in these duties. Moreover, she did all this in exile from her country, friends, family, community, customs and traditions. Even the language was difficult for her.

Loyal to her oath of service, Mother continued her organizing and outreach social activities. Our home was always a refuge for political exiles from Poland, who stayed for days or months until they were situated on their own.

And so it was that issues created in the past – difficult upbringings, as well as wartime injuries of all types – were never dealt with. Instead, they were magnified and carried forward... and handed on to children.

EIGHTEEN

A Polish Upbringing

IN THE SUMMER, OUR PROPERTY WAS A SITE FOR POLISH SCOUT camps, where hundreds of children would come for two to four weeks to be inculcated with patriotic ideals. They socialized with other Polish children, learned the history, customs, traditions, perfected their language, sang songs around campfires, and learned discipline, toughness and survival skills. My parents were helping to raise the next generation of Poles, who would return someday to a free Poland to replace those murdered during the war and subsequent Nazi and Soviet occupations.

My sisters and I were a part of these activities, of course.

After a few years, however, I did not want to go to camp anymore. The atmosphere was too militaristic, the emotions too raw, too intense. Some of the leaders were concentration camp survivors, all had lived through the horrors of war and the German occupation.

My mother said it was up to me, but when I tried to quit a silent wall of resistance rose. First, there was my intense guilt at the betrayal of my duty. Then there was the silent criticism at "shirking of responsibility" that came from the rest of the family, together with the implied pity from friends for my mother, who was such a perfect model and did not deserve such a failure on the part of her oldest daughter.

If my parents seem uncaring, that was not true. In fact, Mother was a warm, loving, caring, unselfish person, highly altruistic, with a strongly developed sense of duty and responsibility. She was a highly respected and much loved scout leader, who lived her life according to her high ideals. As a young girl she had taken the scout pledge:

With a sincere heart and of my own free will, I pledge my life to serve God and Poland, to bring willing aid to my fellow man, and to obey the Scouting Law.

Thousands of young Poles, including myself at age 11 had taken this vow. Few were faithful to its spirit in their lives. My mother was, at least in all essential aspects.

The sad thing is, that perhaps because Mom had never experienced warmth or love as a child, she did not know how to express it to her own daughters. I knew in my head without a doubt that Mom loved me, but I never felt or experienced that love. There was no closeness. She did not cuddle or comfort me as a young child, and was not someone to whom I could confide my fears and worries. It was hard for her to trust her maternal instinct. Her primary loyalty was always to Dad and she followed his lead.

In America, Mother was so overwhelmed by the demands of a life for which she was totally unprepared, and the urgent emotional needs of so many unfortunates she ministered to, she had little time and less energy left for us, especially me.

My Dad was the oldest of five siblings born to a successful, self-made businessman. Grandfather was ruthless in pursuit of wealth and power. He made a small fortune supervising the building of the first railway from St. Petersburg to the port of Murmansk, until the Russian revolution of 1917. He carried out a spectacular, last minute escape from the revolutionaries and returned to Poland with his wife and young son. My Father, born in Russia and taken care of by Russian nannies, was bilingual by the time of their return.

Back in Poland, Grandfather invested his money well. He purchased a large estate including a village, forests, arable land and a small mansion surrounded by 4,000 acres of parkland with a lake, where family and guests enjoyed boating. He converted the arable land to a sugar beet plantation, eventually built a sugar factory and his fortune grew into a large one.

To Grandfather's dismay, Dad was not interested in business, making money or success, but rather in nature and ideas. Instead of a business degree, he got one in forestry. He was interested in plants and animals and given the right circumstances might have become a scientist, as he was more at home in the world of ideas and experimentation than that of action. He had very strong beliefs about fairness and justice. He was an idealist and a big disappointment to his Father, who did not hide his feelings. Nevertheless, as the oldest son, he was raised and groomed to be the heir not only to an estate and a huge fortune, but to a lifestyle, as well.

My Father was born in 1916, two years before Poland regained independence after one hundred years of being cut into pieces by Germany, Russia and the Austrian Empire, and after three bloody and unsuccessful uprisings. It was a time of patriotism, nationalism and heroism. In 1920, when attacked once again by the enemy from the East, the under-equipped and poorly trained Polish volunteer army much to the amazement of the world, beat back the Russians in a battle known as the Miracle on the Vistula. The slogan of the day was "Poland for the Poles," and anyone who was a patriot was prepared to fight and to die in defense of the hard won independence. That was the political climate during Dad's childhood and adolescence.

The social climate was very similar to that of England in the Twenties. The class system was very much alive though things were starting to change. There were the old aristocratic families, still preserving their wealth, and those who had lost it but would always be part of the upper classes. Dad's family came from the gentry - lesser nobility, that large class that for centuries had the power to vote, theoretically equal to the aristocrats and above the merchant, craftsmen and peasant classes, who could not. The reality was that all titled aristocrats were in a class of their own, above the rest. Even among the untitled gentry there were class distinctions. Which is why my maternal Grandmother looked down on Dad's wealthy family and felt my Mother, coming from a poor, in comparison, but socially "higher placed" family had committed a "mésalliance" by marrying Father. Even after moving in with us in America, she continued to look down on him, and refused to eat with us because our manners were not up to her standards. Such undercurrents formed a background to my growing up years.

Dad's health was a major issue during his entire adult life. In his early twenties, captured and held in a prisoner of war camp, he dropped in weight from 175 pounds to 125, over a period of a few months. After escaping, he was so ill, he was not expected to live and was given the Last Rites of the Church. He did recover, but his health was forever undermined. Then came the war, during which he was wounded, and immediately after, he became ill for over a year with agranulocytosis, an incurable blood disease. Again, he was expected to die and received the Last Rites. After another miraculous recovery, he lived until late seventies, when he died of massive heart disease. His entire life he would be sickly, physically weak and plagued with attacks of dizziness and feeling faint due to a brain tumor that remained undiagnosed until his old age.

When I was a young child, in Poland, he had been fun. He would come to the nursery to read stories, watch me make towers from blocks or encourage my laborious rows of letters on construction paper. Immediately after the war, when I became difficult, he was too ill to discipline me so my memories of him, from this period are warm.

After he was nursed back to health at the start of the war, Dad lived in the family owned apartment house in Warsaw. He had a small efficiency, and when they married, Mom moved in with him. Like all his siblings, he had free lodgings and a stipend on the condition that he did not take outside employment. Grandfather, the Patriarch of the family, could afford to support his five grown children and their families. In return, he exercised complete control over their lives. After I was born, Mom wanted to move away, to have her own home and life, but Dad could not make, what would amount to an open break with Grandfather.

When we arrived in America, everything was changed. With Grandfather an ocean away and communications severely restricted, Dad was now the undisputed Patriarch, the head of his small family. As he used to tell us, the family, like the Church, is not a democracy. Indeed, our family was an autocracy and he was the undisputed ruler, just as his Father had been before him. His word was law, and any argument resulted in punishment or at the least a rebuke. Dad was not a mean or harsh person, but never having had the opportunity to learn a balanced exercise of leadership and power, finding himself in a foreign environment fraught with unknown perils and responsible for the safety and survival of his family, he went to the extreme of despotism. Rules were rigid and he was intransigent in enforcing them.

Raised as a member of the European gentry and true to his background, Dad was a perfect gentleman and quickly gained the trust and respect of his new community. He was a perfect host, though without a staff of servants Mother did all the work. He was not to be contradicted or challenged. His daughters were expected to be above reproach, well-mannered, better educated, smarter and a step above the 'commoner', with whom they did not associate. We were expected and raised to be ladies.

He adored my Mother, and she, starved for the love she never got in her own growing years, adored him as well. He was the sun around whom our little family revolved. His needs always came first. Having lost their moorings, my parents had only each other to cling to for comfort and love. It was clear to me as a child, that neither I, nor my two younger sisters were anywhere near as important to them, as they were to each other. From the way they acted and the sacrifices they made for us I *understood* that they loved us, but I never *felt* their love in my body, in my heart.

So along with the anxiety I carried, I was also lonely, craving some of that love my parents had for each other. Still, I held no resentment. I thought that was how it was meant to be. Children were not important like the parents. And I had a future ahead. Someday, I would marry and my husband would adore me. Someday, I too, would be number one in someone's heart. Following Mom's example, I would be the perfect wife loving and taking care of him. Always being there for him, as he would always be there for me.

Whereas, Mom was a shadow being for me – a good, warm presence, more angelic than real -- Dad, on the other hand, was a giant and very real presence in our lives.

Despite his health problems, he liked and regularly engaged in hard physical work. He cleared the trees, which grew up to the windows of our house when we first moved in. Over the years, he dug out the entire cellar by hand, shoveling the dirt and stones on wheelbarrows and pushing them out to the fields where he emptied them before returning for another load. If a rock under the house was too big to remove, he would use small sticks of dynamite to break it up. He was a tough, inde-pendent, do it yourself man, and he expected his daughters to be the same. We would have to help with the clearing and digging, when we were not doing homework or other chores. After lunch, he would often 'invite' guests for some exercise in the cellar. Dad was extremely nervous and tense and the physical exertion seemed to relax him. He enjoyed it, and believed in the dictum: 'Mens sana in corpore sano'.

He was a perfectionist, hard on himself and others.

"A thing is not worth doing if you don't do it well," he would tell us.

Praise was not dispensed at all, on the premise that children were spoiled by it. Criticism was frequent and devastating. I once asked how was I to know he was pleased if he never said so, and he answered that if he didn't say anything then I could assume he was not displeased. I remember standing before him as a young girl in a new dress or hairdo, vainly waiting for him to notice or comment.

"Dad, how do you like my new dress?"

"Is it new?" He would ask. "I hadn't noticed".

"Well, how can I tell if you like something if you never say so?

"If I don't say anything, you're fine. If not, you'll be sure to hear about it." And I always did.

I desperately tried to please him, to get his approval. In seventh grade, I received a prize for achieving the second highest average in the school. Proudly, I brought the book I was awarded to Dad. Knowing the high value he placed on education and performance, I expected praise, but his comment was: "If you try a little harder, next year you could be first."

I realized then that I could never please him, and so I stopped trying. I never again achieved an award.

The qualities that I admired most about my Dad were his principles, his integrity, his sense of responsibility and honor, and his commitment to duty. I prided myself on trying to live up to them in my own life. But, it was not easy.

I learned from him the difference between "want" and

"need." Once, I asked for a new pair of shoes, which I needed for a social function at school. Dad pointed to my feet.

"What's that on your feet?" he asked.

"Shoes," I replied.

"So, you don't *need* shoes. You just *want* another pair."

"Dad, I really do *need* them. There is a party and I can't wear these."

A long lecture followed about destitute children in Africa who have no shoes at all, and who, in contrast to me, did actually *need* them.

"There is an important difference between need and want. Don't forget it," he warned.

On that occasion, Mom intervened privately and I got the shoes. But I remembered, and later in life often felt guilty wanting things I didn't really need, while those who were truly in need went without.

There was, at least for me, the oldest child of whom so much more was always expected, a darker side. On rare but memorable occasions, when Dad felt the sum of my transgressions had crossed the line, he would resort to what in those days was not considered inappropriate. He would spank me. Beside the fact that today we would call it beatings, as I was left with bruises lasting for days, there were serious psychological issues that left a mark on me.

Dad believed in self-control, and never punished when angry. So the violent punishment was coupled with a coldness and deliberation, which felt cruel. He once said while hitting me: "It hurts me more than you," which was the ultimate insult and denial of the reality of my feelings.

I unwittingly provoked Dad by questioning his decisions and arguing, when I felt they were unfair. This was a challenge, and not permissible. Then was the issue of responsibility, which I repeatedly failed by not being able to perform the tasks I had been assigned. I ended up avoiding all responsibility as best as I could. When my daily chores required my presence in the house at a certain time, I would disappear hours before with a book into a cave far enough away from the house to claim not hearing Mom calling me. There, in my safe secluded spot, I would happily read for hours. I would arrive home, finding the table set, or laundry folded and with fake chagrin would exclaim, "I was supposed to do that. Thanks, Helen, for doing it for me."

"I don't mind," Helen would always say. Helen continued to be the perfect child, always asking Mom if there was anything she could do to help. Unlike me, she really did not seem to mind.

The punishment I remember most vividly was the last one I received.

I was about ten years-old and playing with my two younger sisters in the living room, which contained a desk and a swivel chair. We had great fun turning the chair round and round until I got tired of the game and sat down. Helen was spinning Anne, at the time around six, and they were shouting in glee. Suddenly, the chair collapsed and Anne, falling to the ground, began to shriek. Apparently, Helen had been spinning the chair in one direction, and the top came unscrewed. My parents rushed in and seeing Anne crying in a heap on the ground with the heavy chair in pieces, were terrified that she was hurt. After they made sure she was only frightened, Dad grabbed me by the arm and told me to come with him.

I knew what was coming and, terrified, kept saying, "Dad, dad I didn't do anything wrong. We were just playing and having fun, I didn't know we shouldn't do that...."

"Well, you should have known," he replied.

"We were all playing together. Why do you always punish me?"

"Because you are the oldest and should know better."

Mother was standing by the door and I desperately reached for her. "Mom", I cried. But she turned away.

Dad dragged me into a bedroom and started hitting hard.

I was determined to save my pride and not cry, but quickly the pain proved beyond my endurance. I broke down, but my sense of injustice and powerlessness became linked with anger.

"I hate you, I hate you, and I wish you were dead," I sobbed.

He left me sobbing my heart out on the bed, but not before taking away the doll I had been clutching for comfort. "You can leave your room when you are ready to apologize," he said closing the door.

I was in such a state of emotional overwhelm I felt like my brain had evaporated and I was unable to think. All I felt was pain, physical and emotional. I didn't understand what I was to apologize for. I felt completely alone. I wanted to die.

Finally, my sobs subsided and I fell asleep. I woke in the dark, and through a slit of light entering under the door I saw someone had left a tray of food for me. Just the sight of food made me feel like throwing up, and I cried myself to sleep again.

By the next day, I was hungry and ate some food. In the distance I heard the sound of voices, but that only increased my sense of isolation. For my family, life went on as usual, while I was suspended in some weird unreality, totally separate and apart from them. I didn't even have a book to read, which would have allowed me to escape into an imaginary world less harsh and painful than my own. After two days, the loneliness and boredom became intolerable, and I gave up. I apologized just to escape the solitary confinement.

This experience had a profound and lasting effect on me. For the first time, I experienced conflicting emotions: I loved my Father but hated him as well for the violence he inflicted on me. I could not feel safe with him. Nor could I look to Mother for protection: I blamed her for letting him do this to me. I could not trust the ones I loved to keep me safe. This was an echo of the childhood experiences where I first learned parents were powerless to keep me safe from violence during the war. Now, they too had become a danger. They too were the 'bad guys' who might hurt me, and whom I had to fear. From that point, I no longer trusted even those I loved to be there for me, protect or support me, and I no longer trusted promises made or implied in a relationship.

Less dramatic were the purely psychological punishments. We always celebrated Christmas the traditional Polish way. The eager children would watch for the first star in the evening sky. That was the signal for the beginning of the festivities. The family exchanged holiday wishes sharing the Christmas wafer, then sat down to what seemed to the young ones like an endless meal. It was only after it was finally completed, that we settled in front of the lighted tree and sang carols waiting with great anticipation for Santa.

One such Christmas, when the gifts were distributed, each of my sisters had the usual large mound of surprises: dolls, toys, games. I had only one small package to open. "There must be more," Helen whispered. But there wasn't. That year I was a bad girl, evidently undeserving of Christmas presents, so all I got was a pair of mittens. Generally, clothing items were considered necessities and not gifts. It was the equivalent of receiving a lump of coal. I felt a lump in my throat, but all I had left was my pride. I wasn't going to let them know how disappointed and hurt I was, so I made a big show of admiring the hated gift. "Just exactly what I needed," I enthused. "Just what I was hoping for," I lied.

I cried that night in my pillow, when no one could hear. I was nine years old.

In retrospect, I came to realize, that my parents were trapped by circumstances completely beyond their control. These circumstances determined who they were, their value and belief systems and their way of living and raising their children.

First, was the intense atmosphere and environment both political and social where they were raised, and in which and lived their young adult years. I have already described that briefly. Then came the trauma of the war itself and on its heels the trauma of exile.

It is inevitable that unresolved trauma will perpetuate itself and affect future generations. Unless the trauma is healed, traumatized people will traumatize others. This is inescapable. My sisters and I were all traumatized by our parents and by the circumstances in which we were born and raised. The effects for me were growing fear, anxiety, wariness and a sense that I was alone in the world, that I could only depend on myself, that no one was there for me.

NINETEEN

Fear, Courage and Duty

As long as I can remember, I struggled with fears. I was scared of the dark. Helen always would go ahead of me into a dark room to switch on the light. My parents, like most people of that time, were not psychologically sophisticated and had no understanding or sympathy for my feelings.

"Courage doesn't mean not being frightened of danger," Dad would tell me. "It means doing what must be done despite the fear."

It was cowardly to do otherwise, and he expected me to face my fears, to be brave, not a coward. Yet every time I tried and went into a dark room, my heart started pounding in my chest as if it would burst, my breathing became quick and shallow and it would take some time after I turned on the light before my physiology returned to normal. In retrospect, I realize that I was having a panic attack, but then no one knew about such things.

I was terrified of being alone. At about age eight or nine, I was sick and stayed home from school. My parents had errands to run and thought nothing of leaving me alone for a few hours. I truly don't know if they knew how frightened I was, and dismissing my fears as irrational thought I would get over them through exposure, or whether they were completely unaware of my feelings. Either way, they left me and my terror mounted. At the time, we lived in a rented house on the extensive campus of the private school my sisters and I attended. Suddenly, I heard strange noises in the cellar, where the washing machine was located. It sounded as if someone had turned it on, but I knew no one was supposed to be home except me. With heart pounding, I raced out the door not stopping to close it behind me and ran the whole way across two athletic fields arriving breathless at school. They were surprised to see me, having been informed by Mom that I was home sick. When I gasped out that someone was in the cellar, recognizing my state of terror they calmed me down with a hot drink and sent someone to investigate. Needless to say, the washing machine was not on, and there was no stranger lurking in the cellar.

Another source of terror were my frequent and vivid nightmares, from which I would awake in a state of panic. The dreams were variations on one theme: someone was coming to hurt me, I tried to run away but I was running on some sort of treadmill and couldn't make any progress. I tried to scream for help but no sound came out of my mouth. It was a profoundly terrifying experience, and if Helen wasn't there to calm me, I would lie trembling for hours, clutching the knife under my pillow, afraid to go back to sleep. These nightmares persisted throughout my childhood and most of my early life.

I was probably about eleven, when I was left alone on a summer afternoon. My sisters and I each had our own bedroom, but Helen and I had long since decided to sleep in one room and use the second as our playroom. The room had originally been a screened in verandah, which Father had turned into a regular room by converting the screens into picture windows. It was in this large, comfortable, bright room, that I sat reading a book anxiously waiting for my family to return.

Suddenly, I saw flashes of lightning and heard rumblings of thunder. It started to rain. I got up and closed all the windows. The lightening and thunder increased. The rain became a downpour and pelted loudly against the window-panes. My alarm grew as the light of the afternoon dimmed and then turned dark. Suddenly, a deafening clap of thunder exploded so close to the house, I jumped up and started trembling uncontrollably.

The first explosion was followed by another, and then another. It sounded like an artillery barrage. Though I was petrified I was also inexorably drawn to the window. Mesmerized and unable to move, with my heart pounding, I watched the darkness pierced by enormous flashes of lightening immediately followed by loud crashes of thunder.

My terror grew and grew until I could not bear any more. It felt as if my whole self was disintegrating, shattered into pieces by what was happening around me. Yes, for me things were falling apart completely, and the center could no longer hold. I was falling apart. I could not even pray. I could only bargain for my life.

"God," I said to the darkness, "If you make this horror stop, I will dedicate my whole life to your service."

It was now up to God, I thought. There was nothing left for me to do.

Just as suddenly as it had begun, the summer storm came to an end. The thunder and lightening ceased, as did the rain. The sky cleared. The light returned and the sun started to peak through. I was saved. I had made an unbreakable promise to God. There was not a shred of doubt in my mind that this had been direct intervention in response to my desperate plea. It was the first time in my life that I had a palpable and direct experience of His presence.

Spirituality and service would always remain an important

part of my life. During my growing-up years, Polish scouting, which emphasized both, played a huge part.

Unlike the softer American version, Polish scouting was tough. We were dumped at the edge of a forest, had to march with heavy equipment and supplies into the wilderness, and when our Leader decided on the camp site, we had to set everything up from scratch. First, working with small axes and handsaws, we cleared an open space in the thick undergrowth. We set up the heavy tents on their wooden frames. In the 1950s, there was no nylon cloth or light aluminum frames. The tents were simple: no floor, no mosquito netting. After set-up, we dug trenches around the perimeter so as to keep rain-water from flowing inside. Later, we would cut down small trees to make frame beds covered with pine boughs to cushion our sleeping bags. These would keep us a few inches off the ground, so that is the tent did get flooded our cotton, non-water resistant bags had a chance of staying dry. But that was later.

After the tents were up, we got separated into teams and assigned to work details. One team had to dig a latrine, which generally consisted of a hole with a crude log set-up on which we would perch trying not to fall in. Another team built a camp kitchen, and a third organized cooking supplies and our first meal. Others went out on patrol to scout the area and report any apparent dangers. Still others, cut a tree, set-up the flagpole and cleared a circle for the campfire, then went out to gather and cut wood. Finally, a small shrine to the Virgin Mary was erected. There were usually two adults, often in their twenties, and anywhere from twelve to twenty-some girls. Boys had their own separate camps, which worked on parallel lines.

Life in camp was run in quasi-military fashion. Reveille sounded at 6AM, followed by half an hour of exercises and breakfast, after which we dressed in uniform for the raising of the flag. But before that, came tent inspection. We stood in front of our tents, as the assistant commander carried out her inspection. A bed not made to standard, or any type of disorder caused the entire team embarrassment as the offending items got unceremoniously dumped out of the tent for all to witness, followed by a loss of points and the risk getting an undesirable work assignment. The peer pressure was on.

Next came the daily ceremony of the raising the flag. We all stood at attention as our team leader called out our names and we responded, "present". All team leaders then made a report to the Commander. We sang the Polish national anthem and saluted the flag as it was raised. This was followed by a prayer and reading of the schedule for the day. Work assignments were made to the Teams on a rotating basis. These included kitchen duty like cooking meals and clean-up, housekeeping such as latrine duty and general camp upkeep including needed construction and repairs, and guard duty which meant two-hour shifts from 10 pm until Reveille at 6 am.

After we changed into regular clothes, scheduled morning activities began. They consisted of lessons, activities and training for badges, including field exercises. For example, after completing training for the medical badge, the girls would go on a hike. Each girl went alone at timed intervals and followed a trail marked with hidden clues. If she deciphered the clues correctly, she would come across a person, feigning a broken arm or leg, bleeding wound, fainting or other medical emergency. If she responded appropriately, she got points and another clue leading to the next victim. This was all serious stuff, based on the premise that the girls could someday face such a scenario and needed to learn how to cope. There were many badges to be won, some easier and some more fun, but all entailed learning skills.

After lunch there was free time and then games such as volleyball or other fun activities like swimming. Following supper, we washed up and changed into uniform again for the lowering of the flag. We saluted and sang another hymn, this time asking for God's protection for our enslaved country:

> Lord, who surrounded Poland for so many
> centuries
> With the grandeur of might and glory,
> And shielded Her with Your almighty
> protection
> From ill fortunes meant to oppress her.
> Before Your altars we implore Thee: Restore to
> us our free Fatherland, O Lord.

Then we quietly trooped to the campfire circle, and waited for the signal to light it. Seated around the fire, as the flames started to rise we opened with the Scout campfire song remembering days long ago, of knights fighting for our country and warriors protecting her distant frontiers. After this nostalgic and inspirational start, we segued into folk and camping songs, some happy some sad, sometimes broken up by stories or skits. Then came more scouting ones and the inevitable war and soldier ballads of longing, heroism, sacrifice and death. Those were the themes that resonated with me, as those were the feelings ever present in my own heart. Towards the end, the commander gave an inspirational talk. We ended by singing Taps, and walked back in silence to our tents and to bed.

Perhaps once a week, we were woken at one in the morning told to quickly dress and go quietly to the meeting place in the pines. We struggled silently into our clothes and reported half asleep for the night exercises. These were usually games in the forest, such as capture the flag or others in which we were divided into two competing teams. It was all very exciting and fun, but it was not play. There was a sense of serious purpose, as though winning and losing were matters of life and death. The dark forest and the night provided added drama.

My most unforgettable and haunting experience took place when I was eleven and a half years old. It was midnight and I was fast asleep when the team leader shook me awake.

"In your uniforms, Girls. Meeting in front of the tent in ten minutes," she whispered.

"Another night game?" Diana murmured. "We just had one a few days ago."

"Not in uniform, Silly. It's got to be pledge night," Barbara uttered what we all were thinking.

At once, we were wide-awake and filled with tremendous excitement. We all knew that tonight, one or more of the girls in camp would be deemed worthy to take the pledge and ready to take on the responsibility and commitment it entailed. Although I was still young, typically girls were chosen between the ages of twelve and fifteen, I had already attended camp for three years, and was dedicated to serving my country. So, I hoped with all my heart that this would be my night.

We piled out of the tent, and lined up smartly in front. The team leader was waiting, and we followed her into the night. Walking silently by the light of a full moon into the darkness of the forest, she led us on an unfamiliar path. It was a short hike and after awhile, flickers of light appeared through the trees. My heart was beating fast with excitement as adrenaline pumped through my veins.

We arrived on a small clearing brightly lit with a blazing campfire. The other teams were already there. We circled the fire and sang the Scout hymn, then stepped back leaving an open space in front.

"As you all know," the Commander began, "this is a sacred occasion. Two girls will take an oath tonight, which is binding for life. They will dedicate themselves to serve God and Poland. Let us all pray to support them in their solemn commitment."

We prayed together for God to give them the strength to remain loyal, and perform whatever duties the service might require of them, without hesitation, or anticipation of reward, or regard of the cost to themselves. We finished with a hymn to Mary asking for Her blessing. We still didn't know who the chosen ones were, and a fever of anticipation ran through us all.

The Commander spoke again, in a loud voice: "Krysia and Ewa -- step forward."

We stepped forward, saluted and stood at attention. *It's me, it's me,* I kept repeating to myself in disbelief, while shaking like a leaf. I felt so unworthy, yet so incredibly honored.

Krysia went first, and then it was my turn. I raised my right hand, and repeated after the Commander the same pledge my mother had made many years before:

With a sincere heart and of my own free will, I pledge my life to serve God and Poland, to bring willing aid to my fellow man, and to obey the Scouting Law.

She pinned the Cross on the gray cloth of my uniform, shook my hand, and it was over. I stepped back into the ranks of my Team. We sang a final patriotic hymn and quietly marched back to our campground. All the girls were moved by the ceremony, but I was in an exalted state.

My whole life seemed changed. It now had a purpose that made any burden and sacrifice worthwhile. My life had become worth living. I was now a consecrated soldier committed to living and dying for a sacred cause: God and Poland. I felt so blessed, so fortunate to be in the ranks of such an army, and in the service of such masters, that I was over-whelmed with gratitude. I stayed awake for a long time, thanking God and praying for strength to always do his will.

That experience was by far the most poignant and crucial one of my scouting career. I will never forget it to the end of my days. Though, later, I would understand the pledge differently than I did that night, I would still feel bound by it for the rest of my life.

And yet, understanding, feeling and behavior are different things. My head was already in the process of being separated from my heart.

My experience of the Pledge was a culmination of many years of intellectual training and emotional experiences, and it would powerfully influence the direction my entire life. It was as if the rudder and sails had now been set, pointing me to the pursuit of justice and truth. Those were the things that occupied my mind and that pained my young heart. It was nor fair or just that the Gestapo had tortured and murdered innocent people, it was not right that anyone, much less old people, women and children were torn from their homes and lives and treated like sub-humans in concentration camps, it was not fair, just or right that the Soviets massacred 22,000 unarmed Polish officers in the Katyn Forest and the world refused to make them accountable denying even the solace of closure to their families. And it was not fair that I had lost my beloved homeland.

Taking the Pledge, intensified the already powerful feelings of patriotism and desire to dedicate my life to a cause greater than my own self-interest. My nostalgia and yearning for what had been lost and destroyed was assuaged by this commitment to service. It gave a deep meaning and purpose to my life.

My nostalgic feelings were powerfully enhanced by the music I preferred and the books I chose to read. Chopin's preludes, nocturnes and concertos, which I would play endlessly on our hi-fi, were replete with sadness and longing for the same homeland I was mourning. Opera, which I also liked, was full of romantic themes: loss, betrayal, heroism and death.

My favorite book was the *Trilogy*, a three-novel Polish national epic. The author wrote it during another unhappy time, when Poland was partitioned by its neighbors and dismembered as a nation. He dedicated it to the "lifting of hearts' of the oppressed people. For over a hundred years, it would hold the place of honor in the hearts of Poles, as it tells a tale full of heroic struggles both external against invading enemies and internal against the pride, greed and lust for power that destroy nations from within. Patriotic heroes, after great sacrifices and heroic feats of courage, are rewarded in the end, or perish tragically. Men are driven to the depths of depravity by unbridled ambition, and others -- like characters in a Greek drama -- descend into darkness almost by accident of fate, they are all portrayed in real life colors. The book is inspirational and it nourished all my idealistic dreams.

My inner life was very intense and often in conflict with the normal needs and desires of a growing child and adolescent. The desire for fun and play, the pursuit of approval and love, were secondary to duty, which always came first and was inescapable. There was no end to duty, therefore little time for anything else. It was hard to play with dolls, when I was so aware that at that very moment people were starving, tortured, killed. The urgent desire on my part for the freedom to be me, and more than anything, to be heard was defined as pure selfishness.

But there was a toll on me, as well.

All this intensity, combined with the fact that many of these conflicts generated a huge amount of stress, seemed to be causing the acute migraines that I started to experience at this time. They would continue to plague me from then on.

The migraine would start with a relentless throbbing in my head, which progressed to sharp pain and visual disturbances including an acute sensitivity to light. The pain was exacerbated by bouts of nausea and vomiting, becoming so severe at times as to render me semi conscious. I would lie in a fetal position, rocking myself and moaning for hours. I could not hold down any drug, and on those rare occasions when I did, no drug offered any relief.

And so, while I was intellectually committed to my sacred duty, the stress it generated began to cause my body to rebel.

Throughout my growing-up years, my fears and panic attacks continued to plague me unabated. I kept trying to overcome them, and through a tremendous effort of will, as I grew older, was able to hide their noxious intrusions as I was very ashamed. To me, they denoted a moral weakness, a cowardice of sorts. So, if I couldn't conquer the feelings, at least I could and did hide them and not allow them to stop me from doing what I had to do. This self-control came at a cost and added significantly to my stress.

At the Scout camp, in the summer of my thirteenth year, I decided to go for the Wilderness Survival badge, because I hoped it would help me conquer once and for all my fears of being alone and of the dark. Dad always said you should face your fears and not run away, so here I was doing just that: facing my demons. This was an advanced badge requiring demonstrable skills in areas such as first aid, knowledge of edible native plants and mushrooms, and skills in using a compass to navigate in unfamiliar terrain among others. Having completed all the requirements, the final test was spending two days and a night alone in unfamiliar woods and walking out with the help of a compass. Of course, like in all scouting activities we had to observe the "no trace left behind" rule.

The candidate was dropped off at the edge of the forest and walked in for a few hundred feet to a spot from which the road was no longer visible. She was instructed to continue walking deeper into the woods, for an hour or more, following a given compass direction, as there was no path, and identifying landmarks on the way. When she found a suitable location to set up camp, she would proceed to do so, then spend the rest of the time as she saw fit, observing nature and preparing to give a full report of the trip and her activities upon return. The following day, she was to walk out to the drop off point on the road using her compass as a guide. We were dropped off early in the morning and the pickup was the following day between three and four in the afternoon. We had only the most basic supplies: compass, knife, flashlight, whistle, line, a small pot and three matches, along with a wool blanket, rain-jacket and change of clothes in case we should get soaked. For food we had a bottle of water, a few tea bags, a few pieces of dried beef, and a small bag of raisins and nuts. The rest we had to gather on our own.

The morning was bright on clear on the appointed day for my bivouac. I was much relieved as we had had intermittent rain and drizzle over the last two days, and spending two days and a night in the woods, under those conditions, would not have been fun. Since the sun was shining, I could hope that the dampness from the previous rains would soon dry making my trip easier and more comfortable.

North-northeast was my appointed direction, and I started walking -- noting special trees and rocks for use as landmarks on the return. The weather was perfect for hiking. The warm sun penetrated the woods making them light and inviting, and the breeze, which blew through the trees and bushes kept the bugs at bay. It was July, too late for blueberries and raspberries, but to my delight I found some bushes of boysenberries, still undiscovered by bears and other creatures, that still had some berries left on their bushes. I picked them all, saving them in my hat for lunch.

After several hours of hiking, the day was becoming hot, the breeze died down, and the mosquitoes appeared. The hilly and wooded terrain I was crossing became difficult to traverse. There was no worn path and I had to cut through gullies filled with undergrowth. Fortunately, I had a big knife, which I used to slash my way through the tangled mass. The compass was taking me up a steep hill, and after some time the topography began to change. The trees became older, larger and the undergrowth thinned making my travel much easier.

After an hour of this I started looking for a campsite, but found no source of water, so I decided to push on, and soon I heard the rustling of a stream. Much relieved I followed the sound and soon found myself on the edge of a mountain brook flowing with cold, clear water.

Immediately I washed my sweaty face and hands, and had a long drink of the cool refreshing liquid. I ate one of the pieces of beef jerky and devoured all the berries. I would forage for some wild food later, but didn't want to deplete my supply until I was sure I could find edibles for supper. After another big drink, even though it was still early afternoon, I set about building a shelter for the night. I wanted to be prepared.

It took longer than I expected. My plan was to locate a suitable tree around which I would erect a sort of Indian teepee from dry logs and fallen tree branches. Finding the tree was easy but locating the logs and branches took a lot of time and energy, as all I had was a knife, with which to trim the fallen logs to size. Logs that were right for the job were not abundant in the immediate vicinity. Finally, I managed a crude construction and used the knife for cutting evergreen boughs to cover the logs and serve as bedding.

By now it was late afternoon and I was really tired, but knew I had to look for supper. There might have been little fish in the stream, but I was not keen on killing them so I went foraging around the camp. I found some mushrooms I could roast on a stick, but nothing else. I did not want to go too far afield as I feared losing my way back to camp.

It was evening before I returned, and hunger was gnawing at my insides. Lunch had been sparse and many hours before.

I cleared a circle for a campfire and surrounded it with stones from the brook to keep it contained. Earlier, I had gathered some dry tinder and small branches, which I now used to build a small fire. Starting fires was a skill I had mastered and, I was able to get one going quickly with one of my three matches. The second one would be for breakfast, and the third, a spare, for emergencies. While the fire was getting hot, I whittled a stick for my mushrooms, and put some water on to heat for tea. Soon the mushrooms were roasting over the fire and the aroma quickened my hunger. I wolfed down two more pieces of jerky and finally, the mushrooms were ready. Never had I enjoyed a gourmet dish more than I did these simple mushrooms. I finished the meal with some nuts and raisins for dessert and washed it all down with some hot tea.

I was warm, full and very tired. I had been so active and busy all day that I had not had the time or luxury to think or worry about anything.

Now, as I sat back relaxing near the fire, a sense of anxiety suddenly enveloped me. Here I was, all alone in a wild forest with darkness about to fall. *If something happens and I have to scream for help, no one will even hear me.* It was a frightening thought. But darkness comes late in July, and I had another two hours before nightfall.

I knew that if I sat there for two hours, my fears would escalate into a full-blown panic attack, and that prospect was frightening. So I forced myself to get up, bank the fire and scout around the camp for animal tracks. Around the brook, I found raccoon, bobcat, coyote, lots of deer and some others I could not identify. I followed the deer trail a long way, knowing I could retrace my steps, until I lost it in a thicket. The coyote had run along the brook for a while and I could see its marks plainly but then it crossed the shallow water and not wanting to get wet, I did not follow. Fortunately, the breeze picked up again, and the evening air cooled so that mosquitoes were not a problem.

By now it was almost ten o'clock, and darkness began to fall.

On returning to camp, I was so exhausted that I sprinkled some water on my face and, not even bothering to brush my teeth, wrapped myself in the wool blanket, took off my shoes and using my jacket for a pillow fell on the bed of pine boughs. I was asleep instantly.

In the dead of night, the sound of dogs barking woke me, and I sat up with a start. My heart hammering in my chest. Dogs meant people and people meant danger. Especially in the forest, in the middle of the night. The full moon cast a white glow over the landscape as I shakily checked my watch: 1:20 am. July was not hunting season, and anyway hunters don't use dogs at night, I thought. I felt the chill of the night air and pulled the blanket around my shoulders.

Breathe, breathe, I told myself. *You need to be calm and smart. Don't panic.*

But the frightened part of me was shouting, *They're coming to get me, I can't get away, I'm so scared.*

My rational side argued back – in voice that seemed to speak of a night long ago. *Stop it, stop it. You don't know who they are. They probably don't know where we are and won't find us in the dark.*

No, the dogs will find us! I'm so scared. We should never have come here. We will die here.

"We will fight," I whispered to myself, clutching my knife.

I listened intently with every fiber of my being, trying to determine the direction of the sound and whether it was coming closer. It was still some distance away. There was something strange about the bark, not like the sound of dogs in pursuit of prey. It was more like a series of short barks that turning to yelps. Then it became a long, haunting howl.

Instantly, I recognized what it was. I let out the breath I'd been holding and sensed my body relax. These were not dogs. These were coyotes and, judging by the yelps, travelling with pups.

I was a country girl, raised at the edge of the forest by a Father who knew a great deal about animals and passed his respect for them and skill of behaving around them to me. Visitors from cities would wonder at my spending whole days alone in the woods filled with all kinds of wild animals. "Aren't you afraid of bears?" they would ask.

But I wasn't afraid – not of animals. I knew that wild animals were not looking to attack me, and that as long as I took care to stay out of their way, not to surprise them into feeling cornered, I had nothing to fear. It was not wild animals that frightened me.

It was human beings.

As soon as I recognized the howl of the coyote, I knew I was safe. My body though was thoroughly aroused and the adrenaline was still flowing in my blood. It would be hard to get back to sleep right away, so I sat for a long time looking out at the moonlit night and listening to the magical sounds so different from those heard during the day. The birds were all asleep, except for the owl, whose periodic hoots sounded like a mysterious call. The moon had set and I lay down again, in the pre-dawn darkness, hoping to get some rest before morning.

A few minutes passed, and I was half-asleep… when I heard the footsteps.

My eyes flew open, and wide-awake I grasped my knife. But I was so tired, so exhausted from the previous episode I could not even sit up. I lay curled into a fetal ball, cold as ice and completely immobilized by fear. All I could do was grip the knife and, with hearing in hypersensitive mode, listen to the approaching footsteps. This time there was no internal dialogue, no plan of defense, no thought of action. My energy was completely spent and I just lay there waiting for what was about to happen.

The footsteps were coming closer and closer until they stopped just outside the lean-to. In the dark I could not make out the shape, but there was the strong sense of a physical presence.

I will kill myself, if he comes in, I thought, pressing the blade close to my chest. This desperate thought calmed me a bit, and I kept waiting. I held my breath.

We stayed poised there, I and my adversary in complete silence, as if waiting to see who would make the next move.

At length, I heard a rustling noise and the steps walking away, eventually fading in the distance. I didn't make a move or a sound for a very long time. It was not until the morning light appeared and the birds started their chorus signaling the start of a new day, that I finally fell into a fitful sleep.

When I woke up, in a haze from the interrupted sleep and emotionally draining events of the night, I realized that it was late morning. Quickly making a fire for a cup of hot tea, I tried not to think about what had happened and how terrified I had been. The day was bright and sunny and I had work to do. I would have to break down my lean-to and scatter the logs and branches as if they had never been picked off the ground. Not feeling hungry, I drank two cups of tea and making up for the previous evening, brushed my teeth and washed up scrupulously in the cold stream. This woke me up completely and restored my lagging energy.

First, I had to clean up the site of the campfire, as it had to be entirely cleaned up and extinguished. The stones ringing it were taken back to the brook, and the small site itself was soaked with water, and finally covered with twigs and leaves. Pulling the lean-to apart was easy. The harder part was dragging the logs to various locations where they would blend with the natural landscape. By the time the job was finished, the sun was well past noon. I ate the remainder of the jerky with the nuts, saving the raisins as emergency rations for later. My gear was already packed in my knapsack, and after replenishing my supply of water I started the trek back to civilization.

Since I had hiked North-northeast yesterday, the direction back would be South-southwest. Although I had carefully noted landmarks along the route, I was glad I could follow the compass as my mind and memory well still quite foggy from the previous night. Following the compass was not difficult, and from time to time I recognized the landmarks I had noticed before. I came to the pick up point about half an hour early, and stayed concealed until the appointed time.

The Leader, who met me, asked if all had gone well, and I replied in the affirmative. She congratulated me on successfully completing a difficult trial.

I was so happy, so very happy that I had persevered despite my fears. I was truly proud of myself. When friends would ask if it had been scary, I would say, "Sure, it's always scary to be alone in the woods at night."

But I did not elaborate. In telling the story of my adventure first, at the campfire and then at home, I never recounted the true events of that night. I was ashamed of my fear.

Looking back later I would see that I was experiencing very typical post-traumatic stress reactions in my physical and psychological being. Post-traumatic Stress Disorder (PTSD), earlier labeled in combatants as 'Battle Fatigue', is now recognized in psychology as a serious condition that can affect not only soldiers, but anyone who has been exposed to severe trauma, and where they were intensely fearful, vulnerable and helpless. PTSD has an adverse impact on the quality of life, impeding success in interpersonal relationships and work, while also causing a loss of interest in activities previously enjoyed, an emotional detachment and numbness. It affects the personality causing irritability or angry outbursts. It often goes together with anxiety, depression or substance abuse. The three main kinds of symptoms, which characterize PTSD, are: re-experiencing the trauma in the present, avoidance and increased arousal. I experienced them all.

Severe emotional trauma has pervasive, negative developmental effects on young children and adolescents. Traumatized children and adolescents frequently become preoccupied with danger and vulnerability, sometimes feeling imperiled in situations that are not threatening. It undermines their sense of security and the trust that parents can and will protect them. In me, it thwarted the sense of adventure and made me overly cautious, risk averse, afraid to try something new. It also made me hyper-vigilant, afraid to be alone and fearful of abandonment.

Numerous studies have shown that parents suffering from PTSD themselves, as mine did, cannot respond appropriately to their child, or his/her reaction to trauma. And, that failure to provide treatment for children who were traumatized, often leads to PTSD in adulthood.

A common feature of PTSD is the intrusive re-living of past traumatic events, which are experienced as if they were happening in the present. This triggers all the emotional and physiological responses that were associated with the original trauma.

For me, the physiological responses included: palpitations and accelerated heart rate, trembling and shaking, shortness of breath, chest pain, and nausea. Psychological symptoms of increased arousal, which I routinely experienced in these episodes, were: difficulty concentrating, exaggerated watchfulness and wariness, irritability, difficulty falling or staying asleep and being easily startled. Such episodes, in effect panic attacks, become self-perpetuating, as there-experiencing of the trauma in real time had the effect of re-traumatization. During the episodes all I felt was fear intensifying into terror.

Like many people with post-traumatic stress disorder, I repeatedly re-lived the trauma in the form of nightmares at night and panic attacks during the day. I tried to keep them at bay by avoiding any stimulus that might trigger them. To this day, I don't watch movies or read books that describe or depict graphic violence. This eliminates all war movies, documentaries with violent scenes, and news stories showing victims of violence even if the violence was unintended. This is annoying to my husband and friends who sometimes wish to share a show, but for me such topics are too frightening and painful. I was over-sensitized to pain to such a degree that when I see someone, even an animal suffering, I experienced the pain in my own body.

Of course, any talk about "The War" or about the Holocaust was strictly off limits for years. By practicing avoidance, I tried to navigate the minefield of nightmares and panic attacks, which were destroying my life.

TWENTY

Values

WHEN IT CAME TO ACHIEVEMENT, ESPECIALLY WHERE MY father's expectations were concerned, there was no let up. Dad pushed me to excel in every way, and education was no exception. While I was expected to do well, I was also expected to do it faster than others. I had skipped a grade in elementary school and graduated at twelve-and-a-half, the youngest in my class. My parents struggled financially to send me to an excellent boarding school, Westover School for Girls. At first I hated going because I felt it was a new abandonment... being sent away from home. But I ended the first year loving it. The philosophy of the school was to graduate young ladies, who were self-sufficient and independent individuals.

For me, it was the first whiff of potential freedom -- and the beginning of a slight resistance to my parents' pressures... a resistance, which would eventually flower into something else.

My parents loved me. They had unknowingly prepared me for life in the only world they knew: a world of the past, their world, and not the world I inhabited. Still holding on to the dream of going back, they tried to pass on to us the aspirations and goals befitting a time in history that had vanished with the end of WWII. I can see that clearly now.... of course, I did not see it then. All I felt was the need to pull away.

My parents were exiles and suffered that trauma which Armstrong describes so well:

"The violent upheavals of the twentieth century have made millions of people homeless in one traumatic uprooting after another. Exile is, of course, not simply a change of address. It is also a spiritual dislocation. Anthropologists and psychologists tell us that displaced people feel lost in a universe that has suddenly become alien. Once the fixed point of home is gone, there is a fundamental lack of orientation that makes everything seem relative and aimless. Cut off from the roots of their culture and iden-tity, migrants and refugees can feel that they are somehow withering away and becoming insubstantial. Their world -inextricably linked with their place in the cosmos- has literally come to an end. " Karen Armstrong: *The Spiral Staircase,* p 23-24

Not realizing they were sealed in a time capsule of a time that was gone forever, my parents were unable to experience, appreciate or participate in the evolutionary changes going on in the world. The two World wars changed the world in fundamental ways. While Russia, Germany and Austria expe-rienced major changes as a result of WWI, WWII changed Poland in such fundamental ways, that it became an inher-ently different country from the one they had known and were forced to leave behind.

My parents did not have to process the deep differences between pre-war Poland and the United States. They could just dismiss them as belonging to another culture, another world. They had no desire to become American, so they could ignore and reject such differences. They could also dismiss the radical changes in post-war Poland, which they saw as tempo-rary deviations attributable to the Soviet imposed Communist regime. Their fervent hope was to help reverse those unfortunate deviations when their beloved country was finally liberated and free.

They lived for twenty years, isolated in a bygone era, and raised us longing for a country, which no longer existed. Meanwhile, without skills or models for parenting, they had no one they could emulate or turn to for advice and help. This left permanent scars on me and my two younger sisters with whom I made the epic journey to these shores, as well as on the soon to join us baby sister, born in America, but unable to speak any English when she started kindergarten.

In describing my experiences as a young child, I may have painted a distorted picture of my parents. Dad sounds cold and harsh, while Mom sounds indifferent to my distress. Nothing could be further from the truth. Neither of them had had any experience or seen any modeling of childrearing in practice. Just as they were in their childhood, until our arrival in this country we also were cared for and reared by nannies and governesses. My parents suddenly found themselves with three children ages under three to six, who were almost strangers and whom they now had to care for and raise on their own. This would be overwhelming for anyone especially in the difficult circumstances they faced.

It is necessary to remember that child-rearing practices in those days were much different from modern ones. Children were fed, diapered, held and put to bed on a schedule, which was not deviated from or adapted to suit individual needs. The crying baby was not comforted for fear of spoiling it. Children were disciplined 'for their own good.' It was the responsibility of a good parent to raise a well-disciplined, responsible child, who would become a good citizen and contribute to society. Happiness of parent or child was not part of the equation.

Whatever my parents did, they did in the belief that they were doing the right thing. They never shirked their duty, and it was their considered duty to raise their children well. To that end they made many personal sacrifices. They both truly loved us even if they did not know how to show it, and feared that any display of affection or approval would spoil us and make us self-centered or morally weak. Despite many painful mistakes, their intention was always good and they always did what they believed to be right. That is integrity. I respect and love them for that.

So, while it is true that they loved me and did their best, it is also true that sometimes their best was not good enough, and that the trauma and damage they sustained in their lives, damaged me also. Mother's disempowered feminine energies could not balance the controlling, authoritarian masculine energies embodied in my Father. Her emotional absence left me unprotected to the physical and psychological violence of the unrestrained masculine.

When I was away in college, Mother developed cancer and after several years of illness during which Dad kept me at a distance in the belief that my emotional rawness and intensity were too much for her. She died at home in the arms of her husband and two daughters. I lived in New York by that time –two hours away- with my younger sister. Dad did not inform us of her death until it was over. We rushed home but it was too late. By way of explanation for the late call, he told me: "There was nothing you could do anyway." It never occurred to him that I could have said goodbye. It was many years before I could forgive him, and many more before the bitterness faded. I have never truly come to closure with my Mother's death or the fact that I can never share with her the love we both felt but did not know how to express.

In the end, both parents taught me about responsibility, duty and service to others as well as a love for God. These values and beliefs stayed with me for the rest of my life. Mother's life was undoubtedly a life of service, but I was unable to perceive the deeper meaning. All I saw was the surface: a model wife who worked herself to death in the service of others (though not her children). I did not want to follow her example, and spent my adolescence rebelling against it. Later, after I got married, I would try to emulate her in the hope that this would make my husband put me on a pedestal as, I believed, Father had done for her.

TWENTY-ONE

Rebellion
─────────────

BACK TO HIGH SCHOOL......

I started questioning the blind obedience to the Catholic Church. Although I had a powerful sense of the reality of God, the Church held no meaning for me and I felt more connected to the Divine at the so-called non-denominational (really Anglican) twice-daily chapel services we attended than on Sundays at Mass. The chapel services were simple and short, and the beautiful hymns evoked a numinous feeling in me.

I started reading about different religions. I read the Bhagavad Gita, the Koran, the sayings of Confucius and the teachings of Buddha. Oddly, I did not read the Bible. Perhaps this was because the Church taught that lay people should not read it for fear they would misunderstand and misinterpret. I was only thirteen years old, and I didn't understand much of what I was reading, but I did come to realize that there are many different paths to God. I wondered how it was that most religions believed theirs was the only true one, and came to believe that either none of them was, or perhaps in some strange way, they were all true. I had more questions than answers, but I knew I could never go back to blind acceptance and obedience.

I had come to love Westover, where, for the first time in my life I felt accepted. I was acknowledged as being different, but not rejected for it. In fact, the school paper published an article with a picture of me with a British classmate, celebrating us as the school's "international" students. But Dad was not at all pleased with the school philosophy. He advised the headmistress that it was not his goal for his daughter to become independent of the family, and at the end of the year yanked me out against my will and sent me to a Catholic school.

Since there were no private Catholic high schools in the area, he sent me to an excellent one in Baltimore, Maryland. This was devastating. I was being sent even farther away from home, and I did not want to go to a Catholic school. Since it was a day school, Dad arranged for me to live with a Polish family in Baltimore. He also insisted that I enter as a Junior, so at thirteen-and-a- half I was joining a class of girls sixteen and older.

Despite my fears and negative expectations, the school turned out to be quite wonderful, and I came to love the girls in my class and the nuns teaching there.

But my landlady provided a new challenge for my growing resistance to adult pressuring. She considered herself *in loco parentis*, and tried to control and restrict me in the most inappropriate ways. While I was neither ready nor willing to question my father's authority, there was no way I was going to submit to hers. We had endless fights until I decided to put her in her place once and for all.

During Christmas vacation, I told Father that I wanted to try smoking. He told me it was a filthy habit and that he wished he could break it himself. I pointed out that, nevertheless, both he and mother, as well as the people I lived with, all smoked and I wanted to try it for myself. Furthermore, I pointed out that I was open and honest about my intention instead of doing it like a lot of kids my age in secret. This was an eminently rational argument, and Dad was at a loss. He discussed it with Mother and they decided that it was better if I did it openly, so they gave their unenthusiastic permission.

When I returned to Baltimore I lit up a cigarette. My landlady hit the roof. I told her I had parental permission to smoke. She told me I was a liar and promptly called Dad. He confirmed, explaining his thinking -- and she was furious, telling me I had to do it in my room only. My desk faced the door, which opened on the stairwell. I kept my door open and as soon as I heard my wicked landlady ascending, I lit up, extinguishing the cigarette as soon as she passed my door.

Here was the truth, though. I hated the smell and taste of burning tobacco, and never acquired the habit. The only time I smoked was to get her goat. A will to resist was growing in me.

After graduating from high school, I was scheduled to enter Manhattanville College of the Sacred Heart. I did not choose the college, and I have no idea how I managed to get a full scholarship to that expensive, private Catholic girls' school, but Dad was delighted. He was a great admirer of the Kennedys and the daughters of that family were graduates. I, however, did not want to go to a Catholic college, nor did I want to go to and all girl boarding school. I wanted to go to a European style university. I wanted to go to the University of Montreal, where I had taken a summer course the summer after graduation from high school. The U of M had a department of Slavic Studies, and I wanted to study my heritage, I told Dad. The real truth was that I wanted to be an independent adult. I wanted to live on my own and go to classes with adult men and women.

At first he refused. I was enrolled at Manhattanville, where I would be "finished" as a young lady and meet suitable young men from ivy-league colleges and from a background similar to ours -- one of whom would no doubt become my husband. I lobbied relentlessly, using my well-developed logic to put forth rational, persuasive arguments about my need to deepen my knowledge of Poland and its neighbors. Finally, he relented.

The department of Slavic and East European Studies was mostly populated by adults, working during the day and training for a second career. Many were like my parents, refugees from Communist countries in Europe. There were a very few students in their early twenties, most were in their thirties and older. I was fifteen-and-a-half, had never worked for pay or lived on my own. In fact, I had led a very sheltered life. I thought I was all grown up, but I wasn't. Nevertheless, although Dad was still supporting me, this was my first step out into the world. It was a major step towards independence.

The summer after I started college, there was a huge Scout Jamboree to be held in Michigan. My sisters and I were going and Mother was going also. But a new voice was emerging within me. I told Mom I didn't want to go.

"I respect the goals of Scouting", I told her, "But I just don't like it. And, I really hate camping". My idea of enjoyment was to lie in a cool room reading a good book and listening to great music, not traipsing through hot, humid woods or getting soaked in the rain. I was not adventurous and I did not like physical exertion. The pageantry and patriotic fervor attracted me, and I loved singing at the campfire, but I didn't want to go. After a lot of pressure and emotional blackmail by family members, I caved and did go. But it was for the last time. I never went to another scout camp or event, except as a guest. I was beginning to discover what it was that I wanted and didn't want to do, and starting to assert myself.

I continued to question Church dogma and positions on social issues. At that time contraception and abortion were being hotly debated, as they continue to be to this day. I could not fathom how one could be opposed to both. If people did not use contraception, they would have unwanted pregnancies, which they were forbidden to terminate. They would be bringing children into the world, whom they did not have resources to raise thus depriving them and their older siblings of perhaps the basic necessities of life. The mother's life might be endangered through another pregnancy and she might die leaving young orphans behind. Many unwanted children would be born to suffer. I sought out eminent priests to answer these questions and none, not even the Jesuits at my University, could answer them. They all acknowledged the validity of my concerns and could only advise that we must take Church decisions on faith. This was unacceptable to me and eventually I stopped going to church completely, except when visiting home. I knew how painful my decision would be for Dad, and did not want to hurt him.

By the time I was eighteen, I gave up the religion I was raised in and the life-long commitment I had made to Scouting. But I did not give up patriotism or national pride. Patriotism and my lost homeland confirmed my identity as an exile, validating the sense of alienation and nostalgia, which permeated my emotional life. Loss is a "magic preservative," and indeed my romantic yearning for a Poland that no longer existed fueled my melancholy.

Now, feelings of deep unhappiness and longing haunted me, as did nightmares and panic attacks. As I entered the adult world, away from the familiarity of home and began to cut loose my moorings I started questioning the meaning and purpose of my life. I was starting to feel completely adrift on a large and uncharted sea.

Although I gave up the Church, I never lost my faith in God or my personal connection to Christ. I didn't pray on a regular basis, and I didn't give Him much thought, so I can't really explain how or why Christ remained an important figure in my life, or why I believed in his existence or divinity. I just did. Perhaps, He was my only anchor; the one who was always there. And, I knew that He would never hurt me, which I was not something I could be sure about with anyone else.

Emotionally I was a child. My traumatic past had stunted my normal psychological and emotional development. Very proud and confident of my intelligence while afraid of feelings and totally disconnected from my heart I related to everyone on an intellectual level. I was unable to be truly close to anyone for fear that they would abandon or hurt me, or that they would be taken away from me. The underlying feeling of fear was so overwhelming it left no room for other emotions. I was always in fight or flight mode, hyper-vigilant and assessing each situation and person for potential danger.

One evening about ten o'clock, I was returning home after classes. The street was deserted and the windows of our house were dark. Evidently my landlady was out. As I stood on the unlit porch fumbling with my key, I heard a motorcycle approaching and broke out into a cold sweat. My heart pounding, I waited for the attack. I heard the dreaded footsteps and a hand over my mouth kept me from screaming. It was my nightmare coming true, the one where I was trying to scream for help but no sound came out of my mouth. Finally, the grip on my throat loosened and I could breathe. The footsteps faded in the distance. I turned the key and stumbled into the house. My landlady returned to find me shaking in the hall. I told her what had happened and she called the police. I begged her not to do it, because although I couldn't admit it to her, I wasn't completely sure whether the incident really happened or if it had been the product of my feverish, terrified mind.

The police came and I told them the story. Apparently, there had been some incidents in the neighborhood with a motorcyclist, so they took it seriously. The next day, I was called into the station to look at a line-up of men all dressed in leather jackets. I never had seen the face of my real or imaginary assailant so I couldn't identify anyone. The whole ordeal was harrowing.

I craved acceptance and love but on a totally idealistic, poetic basis. When young men tried to court me I was totally unaware of their intentions and thought they were just being nice. I considered them good friends, and when they finally made it clear that they wanted more I felt betrayed. I never learned to form peer relationships. I was proud of the fact that young men brought chocolates to my best friend, but flowers and poetry to me.

I had an imaginary fiancé, who was killed during the Hungarian revolution, and whose death explained my constant sadness and disinterest in romantic advances by others. This sounds pretty extreme, and in a way it was. But in another way it fitted my circumstances perfectly. I was raised to play a heroic part in a historical drama. I felt different and apart from others, and I was terrified of intimacy. In some ways, I saw myself as a tragic, romantic heroine to be loved and admired from a distance. This imagined story fit all the requirements: it was tragic, romantic and served to keep others at a safe distance.

By this time, I had developed a strong synesthesia between images and feelings. This meant that the images projected by my mind were immediately infused with very powerful feelings. When I imagined the handsome young man shot and dying for his country's freedom, I immediately felt immense sorrow, grief and love for him. These very real feelings, in turn, substantiated the imaginary scene giving it a strong sense of reality. At times, I would get lost in the reverie and I had to make an effort to remember it was all a painful fantasy, a figment of my imagination. But ultimately, I knew. Though I was playing on the edges of reality I never actually fell off the cliff. I could always bring myself back to reality.

The drama provided me with a heroic context for my life. After my childhood and adolescence, steeped in death, blood and sacrifice, how could I be attracted to a college boy or even man who was living a normal, mundane existence. My fantasy provided the barrier I needed to keep others at bay. Though some young men attempted to break through, the barrier was pretty effective. It is hard to compete against a dead hero.

Fear and avoidance of danger became the dominant drivers in my life.

TWENTY-TWO

Searching for Safety

AFTER GRADUATING FROM COLLEGE, I GOT A JOB IN NYC AND found living alone impossible. Without Helen there to keep me safe, I spent sleepless nights listening to footsteps of men coming to kill me, or slept fitfully to be woken by nightmares. Two men proposed marriage, and as I could not go on alone, I had to choose. One was only a few years older than I, good looking, fun, adventurous and exciting. The other was my office manager, nineteen years my senior, still living with parents, handsome, stable and perhaps most important a WWII veteran. He had a painful past, as I did, and had been traumatized by the war. Though he rarely talked about it, this was a powerful bond for me.

He had a father who wanted him to be different from who he was, and who rejected him in favor of his sisters. I could identify with very easily with that pain. He told me how after being drafted with other men from his class at college, going through basic training together, they were all outfitted to go to the Pacific theatre. On the night of departure, he, alone, was sent to Europe instead. He never understood why this happened and it was traumatic for him to be going into the deadly unknown, separated from his comrades. Nevertheless, he fought bravely and was wounded in the Battle of the Bulge, for which he received a purple cross. As a medic, he risked his life to save or comfort under fire, men lying wounded on the battlefield. All of this made him a hero in my book, though he did not talk freely about it and only shared when I persisted. He had been physically and emotionally wounded in the same war that had emotionally crippled me. He was a sensitive and brilliant man, and as I, in addition to heroism, also highly valued intellectual prowess, of course he was my choice. We were quickly married.

It seemed a perfect choice: I needed an intelligent, powerful "father," whom I could admire and who would protect me. He, in turn, was looking for the perfect mother to replace the one who still cared for him on a daily basis, and who had given him unconditional love from the beginning. I had the potential to replace her. My own mother was a model of such a wife, and through observation I had acquired the skill set -- although I was afraid to follow in my mother's foot-steps too closely. After all she died young of cancer, and her life was not the happy one I wanted for myself. I did, however, want to have the relationship of total commitment and love my parents exemplified. I was willing to give it a try.

By now, I had come to realize that the forced indoctrina-tion in nationalism, religion and the traumatization of my family and the closed society I had been raised in, were at the root of my chronic nightmares and the source of my fears and deep unhappiness. Somehow, I always felt that I was playing a role in a tragedy —it was a noble role, and I was proud it was mine to play. It was my destiny. Something in me also knew the outer world saw things in a different way, so I never discussed this with anyone. Dad had made it quite clear. It was my and my sisters' duty to grow up to be good Polish patriots, devoted to our homeland and ever ready to serve her. But, attempting to play that role was becoming increasingly painful and I started to wonder if perhaps I had a choice.... I knew that my life was not working and that I wanted to do something different.

I knew my life was not working, because I wanted to be happy, and I was not. On the outside, I was functioning on a high level. I had graduated from a good university with an education in the history, literature, culture and politics of Slavic and East European countries. I was fluent in three languages, and could understand, read and write three others. I had gotten a decent job and could support myself.

On the inside, fear ruled my life and prevented me from living as an autonomous adult. I could not live alone. The gap between reality and terror was widening. Having discarded my parents' certainties, I was no longer sure of who I was or where I was going. I realized that, out of the tangle of strong family priorities, commitments, and values I had to separate and discover who I was and what was important to me, in order to find the purpose of my life.

Marriage to an American Protestant was the beginning of a new life, custom designed by me, and totally different from the past. My family would be American, and my husband and I, not my father, would make all the decisions. First, however, I had to somehow get out from under from his control. In order to get Dad's approval for my marriage I had to let him orchestrate the entire wedding. He made all the decisions insisting the one bridesmaid I was allowed to have, an old family friend, whom I did not like and would have never chosen. This was a small price to pay for liberation and a future.

I had hoped my fears would abate as a result of being married, but this did not happen. Our first home was a cute, completely renovated upstairs apartment in a single-family home located in a safe part of the City. It was bright and cheerful with lots of windows and light. Containing a small bedroom, sitting room and kitchen it was cozy and perfect for a newly wed couple.

A few months after we moved in, I came down with the flu

and had to stay home from work. My husband left for the office, and soon I heard the sound of our downstairs neighbors' door being locked. I looked out the window to see them leaving. I was alone in the house.

Trying to get some rest, I lingered in bed, when I heard the footsteps. Adrenaline surged up my body, and I felt the familiar blinding rush of energy to the brain. My brain went into hyper-vigilant status, trying to determine if this was a fight or flight situation. I felt trapped, as the bedroom had only one entrance and exit. And in a split-second I was I hunkered down under the covers paralyzed, shaking and flooded with panic.

The footsteps paused for a while and then resumed.

I remained frozen where I was, trying to figure out where the sounds were coming from, but there was no pattern. They seemed to be all around. It occurred to me that perhaps this might be the sound of hot air in the vents, and that fortuitous thought relieved my paralysis though not my terror.

I jumped out of bed, threw on some clothes and escaped like a shot out of the dangerous apartment. The relief was immediate: sick or not, I was alive and safe. For the moment, I had gotten away.

After an hour of walking the streets, my nerves calmed and my breathing back to normal, I got into the subway and went to the office looking like a ghost. My clothes were disheveled and my hair uncombed, but I did not care. I received some funny looks from my co-workers. As I was already married to the office manager, so no one commented on my lateness or my unkempt condition. I was embarrassed to even tell my husband about what happened so I just said that I felt better and decided to come to work. There was nothing else to do: going back to the apartment alone was not an option.

My husband knew about my fears from the beginning and, having a schizophrenic sister, he was, unlike my parents, aware of psychological issues. But he was not sympathetic either to her problems or to mine. I discovered this in the very beginning. During our honeymoon trip, one night we were staying in a small motel with no phone. Late that evening, we had a bad fight. Knowing full well how terrified I was of being left alone, he stomped out into the dark with the words: "I hope the goblins get you." I knew then, that I could not trust him to stay and protect me. I could not share my panic attacks with him. Again, I became ashamed of my fears, as I had been during childhood and adolescence.

Trying to understand my problems led me to an interest in psychology. I started reading extensively and eclectically in the field. When the book, *Rational Therapy* by Albert Ellis, came to my hands it changed my life. Here was a rational method that could be employed by anyone wanting to stop the repetitious cycle of negativity, which led to misery and despair. The method (a pre-cursor of cognitive therapy and later known as Rational Emotive Therapy or RET), appealed to my strongly-developed logical, rational mind. I could and would do this.

In short order, I mastered the techniques, which consisted of changing my emotional/behavioral response to triggering events by changing my beliefs about the events themselves.

Ellis posited that current emotional problems (such as my anxiety attacks) were not entirely due to past traumatic events, which could not be changed, but more so to current false beliefs, which we had subconsciously developed. He proposed three common negative beliefs and the first one seemed to fit me. My own version went something like this:

I must always perform well and please my significant others. If I fail to meet this sacred goal, that will be awful; it will mean I am a failure, a bad, incompetent person who does not deserve anything good and deserves to suffer. I will be unloved and rejected.

It's not hard to see that going through life with such a belief led to all kinds of misery. I practiced diligently the exercises provided in the book in order to undermine and change these negative beliefs. I kept telling myself that if I truly try hard and fail at something, it will be disappointing and unpleasant but not the end of the world. That making a mistake did not mean I am worthless, a failure at everything and deserving to be punished. By writing down my fears and analyzing them, in time my rational mind started to gain control over the irrational emotions.

The exercise of these techniques reduced to some extent my frightening internal chaos. It put the demons to sleep, and held the panic attacks at bay. Now, I could move on to the next step: getting away from my father's control, so I could finally live my own life.

Still, my personal battles continued.

The most common ways of coping with trauma, I'd learned, are either *turning inward and shutting out the threatening outside* or *turning outward and shutting out the inner torment*. My inner chaos was somewhat diminished and partly under control through the use of RET techniques, which I practiced assiduously. It was now essential to monitor and manage stimuli, which might trigger the panic again.

A major stimulus I needed to avoid was any exposure to violence. Thus watching TV news, especially local ones, was out, as there was a good possibility that a car accident featuring injuries, some violent crime or other aggressive incident would be featured. War movies were off the menu as well, along with any thrillers or shows that included potentially frightening scenes. I was careful to restrict my reading along the same lines, avoiding violence and suspense. "Cozy" mysteries became my fare of choice in fiction.

It was also critical to create for myself a psychic space free of the coercive influence of ideologies, as well as of the ideas and opinions of others. I needed the space to discover what I believed, thought, wanted. I needed a safe space to find myself. Having tamed, or so I thought, the inner demons, I had to keep the outer world at bay. I was turning in and building a security fence to keep others out.

Choosing an American husband had been a first step, as it created an inevitable distance with my family. My new husband, coming as he did from a different culture and being closer in age to my father than to me, refused to accept without question Dad's patriarchal authority. But this was not enough. We needed more distance. We wanted to buy a house, and could not afford anything closer than one hundred miles from New York City. If we went north, to upstate New York or to Connecticut, that would put us close to my family. If we went east to Long Island, that would leave us close to his family and four hours away from mine.

We went to Long Island. By making that choice, I made it difficult to maintain a close contact with my family. Long distance phone calls were expensive and email was years in the future. For many years, we saw each other on Christmas and perhaps once for a weekend in the summer. Our relationship grew distant.

In two years we had a child, and I had created a safety cocoon around our little family. The rare contact we had with either of our families of origin was on our terms. I modeled myself on Mother, and tried to become a replica of the perfect wife. I cooked all our meals from scratch, baked bread, made fresh yogurt and sewed our clothes. My husband loved to fish, and I encouraged him to buy a boat and enjoy his hobby. Although fishing was distasteful and extremely boring to me, I never complained.

After work on Fridays, we would load up for the two-hour trip to Montauk, where our thirty foot Chris Craft was docked. I accompanied him on summer and fall weekends, sleeping in the little cabin, cooking what I could in the galley and reading during the hours he was trolling for bass or blue-fish. My husband was a serious and superb fisherman. He had no interest in going to nearby islands for a hike or picnic. It

EWARE about fishing. He got up at four in the morning, was all that was when the fish were biting and we were back because up at nine. After cleaning and selling the catch, the rest of the hot day was spent sweltering at the dock, while he tinkered with the engine or chatted with the other commercial fishermen. A second foray took place at four in the afternoon, returning at nine in the evening. It was not much fun for me, but that was the unspoken deal: I would keep him happy, while he would keep me safe.

Unfortunately, this became harder on me after we had the baby, but still I went, always trying to be the perfect wife.

Soon we had a second boy and our family was complete. By now, though, serious cracks appeared in our marriage. Although we lived in a family neighborhood, I still had no social skills and did not know how to make friends. I felt awkward and didn't fit in. My background, though now discarded outwardly, continued to haunt me inwardly. There was nothing in it that I could share with my young American neighbors. Nor did their memories and stories ring any bells for me.

Consequently, I found myself more and more alone. I had intentionally isolated myself from my family, my roots and my past. But I could not build a new community where I would belong. I was a young mother, trying to raise two small children in isolation from friends and family. I had no support system and the unrelenting pressure of responsibilities began to mount.

The children -- were the greatest joy of my life. They completely loved and accepted me, and I completely loved them in return. Real love is not based on need, as my marriage was. My sons were the first and only persons in my life I loved truly and unconditionally. That brought a new set of problems.

In my earnest attempts to be the perfect wife and mother I could not reconcile the conflicting needs and demands of my family. Since there were no grandparents, aunts or uncles to fill in, I had to somehow manage it all. But it did not seem manageable, especially when an inner voice whispered in my ear my father's precept: "Everything must be done well, or it is not worth doing."

But how can one tend perfectly or even well to the very different and often contradictory needs and wants of three human beings?

It didn't help that my inclination is to focus on one task at a time and complete it before moving on to the next. It was easy with just one baby. When his brother came along, it became impossible. I started feeling torn in half, always guilty that I could never completely satisfy either one. It was many years later that I learned, when studying child development, that children do not need a great mother... all a child needs is a "good enough" one. This notion, had I understood it, would have comforted me. Instead, I was reading *Magical Child*, by Joseph Chilton Pierce, which talked about what children ideally should get from a parent and how easily they can be damaged when they don't get it. My guilt at my failings as a mother tormented me.

Then one of the demons from the past reared its ugly head.

During my childhood I had suffered many losses. I had heard and read stories of worse ones. Although for years now I refused to watch war movies and avoided news stories or shows containing violence, I had been sensitized to it, and it was always lurking around the corner of my reality. Long before, I had formed a subconscious belief that anything I am attached to, anything I love will be taken away. For this reason I had very little attachment to places or things. I had even discarded my own family, including my adored sister, Helen. But I did not know how to keep an emotional distance from the two little creatures I had carried in my womb for nine months and brought into this world. I loved them so much I could not and did not want to imagine a life without them in it.

I began obsessing about their safety, yet felt convinced I could not keep them safe. I was sure that I would not be allowed to keep them, that I would lose them in a violent manner, and the very thought was enough to drive me insane. These children had brought me so much joy, the only happiness I had ever felt, and the tortured feeling deep inside that I would inevitably lose them was unbearable. They too would be taken away as everything else in the past had been taken from me. Fortunately, I was too busy to brood on these dark forebodings very often. Most of the time, they remained as a constant nagging anxiety out of my conscious awareness.

I lived with feelings of doom, waiting for the other shoe to drop. It was a state of generalized anxiety where anything could become a lightening rod for my fear. When I saw a documentary on the kidnapping of the Lindbergh baby, it triggered many months of unease about the safety of my children. It was not precisely that I feared they would be kidnapped. I just lived in a state of constant apprehension about their safety. Subconsciously, I still felt I deserved to be punished. Until my children entered my life, the greatest punishment I feared was violence, pain and torture. But now everything changed and my greatest fear was any harm coming to them.

The life I had carefully constructed went on, though not as happily as I had intended or hoped. I was desperately searching for love, security and purpose. I wanted to be loved for who I *was* – not, as my father had loved me, for what I *did*. I did not then realize that this wish too led me into a trap. My husband did love me as I was. In fact, we had this unspoken contract: I would never change and he would never abandon me. For a few years we lived in this land of make believe, shutting out the real world and only letting in those who fit into our fantasy. We called it "playing house," a bit like the later Barbie and Ken dolls.

Eventually, however, the marriage began crumbling as I realized that I had exchanged a cage with bars of iron for one with bars of gold. My new cage was infinitely preferable to the old one, but it was still a cage. I was in my early twenties and had a lot of growing up to do. That made change inevitable. As I started to grow, the golden cage became intolerably cramped; it started to feel more and more like a prison. I wanted to do God's will, and I prayed to Christ to show me the way, but He remained silent.

When I was in my early thirties, I had what I consider my second spiritual experience. This experience may sound strange to many readers. Looking back, it sounds strange to me, as well. I can only report it as it happened.

It was a late fall afternoon and I was heading home from town, when the blinding light of the setting sun reflected in my rear-view mirror forced me to pull off the road. It was so strong and brilliant, that it took a few moments to reorient myself even after I had stopped. As the light dimmed, the realization suddenly struck me that I was driving due west and the light had come from behind, directly from the east.

That's impossible, I told myself. *The sun doesn't set in the east.* But the fading light was clearly still shining from the *east*. All at once I knew it was the Light of Christ shining in my mirror. I felt His presence infusing my whole being with a peaceful calm, and sat there absorbing that feeling for a long time.

As a logical, rational person, not given to "mystical" experiences, I struggled with what had happened. I turned the car around and drove back to see if there was anything unusual that could account for my experience. But there was not. Everything seemed completely normal. I still felt the peaceful calm inside and continued home. To this day, I don't have a rational explanation for what happened on that country road. There may be one, but I just don't know what it is.

At the time, this experience did not enlighten me as to my way forward. It did not inform me as to the goals or purpose of my life. Perhaps because from childhood my path had been clearly defined by my Father, once I stepped away, I felt lost. Even though I kept looking for signposts, there were no trail markers in the wilderness in which I found myself. And although this mysterious occurrence did not provide me with guidance, it did leave me with a sense of connection to something greater, a reconnection to my relationship with the Divine –Christ. It left me with a sense of awe that remained with me for a long time.

While terrified of change, my husband recognized he could not hold me back from development and growth. I could not forever remain the twenty-year old girl he had married. I was maturing into a woman and he was not prepared to accompany me on my journey. He did allow me the freedom to explore as long as I always returned to the cage. My explorations were blind shots in the dark, more destructive and painful to us both, than helpful.

I immersed myself passionately in worthwhile causes: social justice, fairness, the anti-nuclear movement, social work. I involved myself in dead-end relationships, harmful to me and hurtful to my husband. I had no idea how to find what I was looking for, but I kept running as fast as I could to stay ahead of the hidden dragons from my past that continued to chase and haunt me.

My well-paying job, which supported a comfortable lifestyle and gave me a sense of independence, was another trap. I had outgrown it also. I did not have the courage to leave the security of the marriage or the security of my work.

TWENTY-THREE

Disintegration

IN THE END, IT ALL CAME CRASHING DOWN. IF ONE DOESN'T make choices in life, sooner or later, life will make choices for you.

As I continued to vacillate, the marriage continued to dissolve until I finally left. Soon thereafter, my job came to an end as a result of a horrible car accident, which left me with a foot and head injury, physically and mentally disabled for a long time. Unlike the break with my childhood and adolescence I had tried to engineer with my first marriage, this, finally, was it: a real break with the past and the possibility for a new and different future.

Although I insisted on and got joint custody, I agreed to leave my two sons with their father, in our home. In fact, I continued to pay the mortgage on the house in order to make the transition less stressful on them. My husband had once threatened that if I ever made him leave, he would go away and I would never hear from him again: the boys would not have a father. I don't know if this was just a threat or if he would have done it, but I did not dare to find out. The boys, I believed, needed their father more than me. He could provide the stability and security, which I could not. My whole life was in chaos and I had no idea where I was going. I knew that whatever happened, I would never stop loving my sons, I would always be there for them in every way I could. I tried to do what was best for them, to protect them.

Subconsciously, I was fulfilling my darkest fears -- my belief that everything I loved most would always be lost to me. I had some control, however. By giving them up, I could protect my children from the violent death through which I believed I would otherwise lose them. Leaving them was the hardest and most painful decision of my life, but the other option was unbearable to even consider.

Although the psychotherapeutic work I had done had diminished my panic attacks, they were only temporarily in retreat. It was a superficial, skin-deep improvement in the symptom, not the true healing that needed to happen. My subconscious fears were still driving my decisions and controlling my life. I was not consciously aware at the time of the terror that drove me to leave my children. I thought and truly believed I was making a rational decision in the best interest of their safety and well being.

At the same time, while grieving for the loss of my sons and my self, I was trying to build a new relationship with the man who would later become my second husband. What I did not recognize was the fact that I had to cling to someone who would offer me some love and protection: a safe harbor.

I tried the same old tricks as in my first marriage: I would take care of his needs and be the perfect wife if he would love me above all else and protect me. But my second husband was a different man, and not willing to play that game. After we were married, he told me if he needed a housekeeper or business manager, he could hire one. He wanted something different from a wife. This left me at a complete loss. I had no models for a different marriage and felt useless since he didn't want the only one I knew.

I was in a no-man's land. I had freed myself from the cages I had lived in since birth, but now I was completely lost. I had no idea how to find the love I wanted or the purpose God had for me. Facing an inner tangle, I was starting to fray emotionally. Getting out of the cage was not enough. I had to heal the old wounds, which were unconsciously continuing to control my life choices and decisions. I had to build new inner structures, which I didn't have. I had to overcome the fear and the sense of powerlessness and worthlessness, which kept me in chains, unable to become fully the person I was meant to be. My husband was not willing to play the game of make-believe, so I now had to confront reality. My reality was not pretty and facing it was not easy. I was overwhelmed by the task facing me.

In the past, I always ran from my problems, and I was good at getting away. Extreme involvement in many good causes kept me too busy and too tired to look at myself and see the inner mess. But now, there was no escape. I lived in a remote area. My health was damaged, which severely limited my mobility and ability to get involved. My husband had his work and I was left to face the pain. Unable to escape into a new round of unending activity to distract me, I felt useless and worthless. The fear heightened and my panic attacks became more frequent. My inner chaos became harder and harder to control. This is what childhood trauma had become so many years later, as my damaged self tried to navigate the adult world.

I could and did pursue my study and practice of psychotherapy. This provided many new insights into my own self. One of my first breakthroughs in untangling my knotted inner life was when I began to learn about the effects of severe or prolonged trauma, and to recognize the fact that these effects described *me*. I learned that:

Trauma is always painful and damaging, leaving us scarred for life. Most people remain stuck in the negative aftermath. But there is a way through it, so that it can ultimately become a path to transformation instead of destruction.

TWENTY-FOUR

Effects of Trauma

TRAUMA CAUSES A TEAR IN THE FABRIC OF OUR BEING. IT leaves a black hole, which threatens to devour us. The goal of life becomes survival. We must at all cost avoid falling into the hole. Falling in and being swallowed by this bottomless pit would mean the total annihilation of our being. The hole causes us endless pain, an existential agony accompanied by relentless fear and terror.

When a fabric is torn, depending on the size of the hole, it might be mended or worked around. The damage weakens the fabric and renders parts of it useless and the whole becomes less valuable or even worthless. When the irreplaceable fabric constituting who we are is torn, our sense of worth is damaged.

Feeling diminished in worth or even worthless is a common result of trauma. To a great extent, this is the result long-term societal attitude toward victims of trauma. Historically, instead of compassionate acceptance and understanding there has been a response of cruel rejection, blame and even punishment.

Women who have been raped are to this day considered in

many cultures to be "damaged goods." Questions are raised about their past, or inappropriate dress, or seductive behavior. The implication is that it was somehow the victim's fault. In some parts of the world, they are rejected by their families, ostracized by society or even put to death.

Until very recent times persons who were handicapped mentally or physically were treated as less than human. They were exhibited in circuses, routinely made fun of and mistreated. They were seen as not having any value to society –worthless burdens. The same is still true of the mentally ill. A recent book tells the story of a young man whose fiancée is diagnosed with schizophrenia. While she is being treated in a residential facility, his friends try to introduce him to potential girlfriends telling him he must move on and assuming a mentally ill fiancée is a non-issue.

For a long time, certain diseases, for example, Cancer and AIDS were considered shameful and people would conceal such conditions as long as possible. Alzheimer's and other forms of senility are shunned. According to some researchers, people respond in one of two ways to news of serious illness in their friends or relatives: they rally or they flee. Unfortunately, most flee. The writer recounted how she told 150 friends and relatives of her mother's advancing senility. Only a tiny percentage responded with offers of help, the rest responded not at all.

Because all those who have suffered trauma were unable to stop it from happening, they are frequently in some way judged for their powerlessness and found wanting. The victims are seen as sharing blame for the crime. They couldn't or didn't do what was necessary to fight or at least avoid the calamity.

Why didn't the girl being raped fight harder, scream louder? Why was she there at all? Was her dress or behavior provocative? Why did the Jews go to the ovens like sheep? Some people ask. Why didn't they fight? They must have been able to do *something*...When asked, "Like what?" they answer that they don't know, but there must have been something. A lot of these feelings are unspoken, but they are there, and the victim is further traumatized by the judgment and rejection.

Effects of trauma are physical and emotional. They affect relationships, career and creativity. And, they affect the entire community, not just the individual. They are like a pebble tossed into a pond. The ripples spread wider and wider covering the whole surface of the water. When twenty six children and adults were massacred at Sandy Hook Elementary, not just their parents and families were affected and in mourning. The entire community was traumatized. After 9/11, not just the friends and families of the victims, and not just New Yorkers, but the entire country was traumatized.

Psychologists know that trauma can become lodged in the nervous system and cause a frightening past experience to be relived again and again. Sometimes the actual event gets forgotten, but the feeling never is, and a new circumstance triggers the paralyzing terror. It is usually completely out of proportion to the precipitating factor, and rather than being a response to the present day trigger, it is an autonomic response lodged deep in cellular memory, which gets unpredictably activated.

That is what happens when war veterans get startled by a loud bang of target shooting, fireworks or the blare of a rock band and respond as if they were back in the middle of a brutal firefight where they perhaps lost friends and comrades. The sound may trigger a flashback bringing back in full intensity the old memory and causing a mental reliving of the trauma. Or, the memory may have become disconnected from the feelings lodged in the body. They may find themselves overwhelmed a state of inexplicable anxiety, fear and sadness, without understanding or being able to explain the reason.

To this day, I avoid watching violent movies or reading thrillers for fear of activating this painful and uncontrollable response. The anxiety, fear and sadness triggered in me far outweigh any enjoyment of the book or movie. Avoidance of triggers is a common coping mechanism and refusing to read certain books or watch certain movies is not that much of a burden. But it can get much more complicated.

TWENTY-FIVE

Coping Strategies and Beginnings of Insight

AVOIDANCE WAS ONE OF MY COPING STRATEGIES. I AVOIDED not just violent books and movies, but many other things as well, which constricted my existence and ability to live a full life. Fear of violence prompted my avoidance of living alone, being alone, going places alone, doing things on my own. Fear of loss made me afraid to travel as that entailed leaving my home and I was never completely sure it would be there on my return. It made me leave my children, because I believed I would lose them otherwise –it was better to have them in my life at a distance, than lose them forever. It caused me for many years to avoid real commitment because I feared I would be abandoned. I avoided taking chances because it was too dangerous.

Another common symptom of Post-Traumatic Stress Disorder (PTSD), which I exhibited, was rigidity of response. Since hyper-vigilance and catastrophizing made everything seem a matter of life and death, a rigid, inflexible response was required. I had to get it right or a catastrophe was bound to occur. I always anticipated the worse case scenario so I could be prepared to act appropriately in any extreme situation. I needed certainty and order. Without it, the outer disorder would trigger my inner chaos. A camp survivor described my reality exactly:

> "And as I spoke I was remembering the concentration camp where chaos had reigned and God had appeared absent and I had never known from one day to the next whether I would survive. Then my memory spun backwards beyond the war -both wars- to my childhood where again I had lived with uncertainty and never known from one day to the next if my strict father would decide to beat me in order to bring me up properly. One had to have certainties otherwise life became hideous, painful, terrifying. Order had to be promoted and defended with tenacity. It was a question of survival." (Susan Howatch: *Absolute Truths*, p.151).

In adolescence, I had trouble expressing or connecting with feelings. When I was about twelve years old, Mother received a letter from my beloved nanny, Danda, who was lost to me in the turmoil of war. She wrote trying to reconnect with me, and explaining what had happened to her.

Liberated by the Allies, she remained for a long time in a refugee camp, until finally she was able to migrate to England. There, along with thousands of other war refugees unable to return to Soviet occupied homelands, she struggled to survive economically. She never gave up trying to find us, and finally succeeded years later. Mother urged me to answer her letter, but I would not. Although at age twelve I had heard the whole story, and knew why she could not come back to me in Warsaw, some part of me felt abandoned and could not forgive. The memory of love and loss was too painful and had to be avoided. I refused to write to her. A few years later, when I heard she had died I regretted my refusal.

By the time I became an adult, I had trouble identifying my emotions. Many years later, my husband asked my why I was so angry. I was shocked that he would say that.

"I'm never angry, just upset." I responded.

My second husband, who is a psychiatrist, said, "Call it what you like. But it's anger."

This confused me, but I started to consider what he said. It took me years to start identifying that particular emotion correctly, and I still have trouble expressing it appropriately. Since most of my life I never consciously allowed myself to feel most negative emotions, I had had no opportunity to practice modulation in their expression.

This lack of skill in expressing emotions caused many interpersonal problems for me. It also distorted my personality development, as I became a person devoid of certain normal feelings. I truly never disliked anyone. Friends thought me naïve and vulnerable. Someone could attack and hurt me, but once they said "sorry," they were completely forgiven and all was forgotten. Of course, as soon as I turned my back, they would stab me again, to my complete surprise. I didn't seem able to learn that some people could do 'bad' things. The memory of 'bad people' was so frightening to me that it had been repressed completely.

The formation of my personality was further distorted by the imposition on me, by parents and the émigré society in which I was raised, of a false identity and a complete rejection of my real self. There was no support or acceptance for the person I really was, so, in order to get approval I learned to be the person I was expected to be. I developed what is called in psychology a false identity or a false self. Whenever my real self rebelled and broke through (like when I expressed my dislike of camping and refused to attend the Scout Jamboree), it was judged, criticized and condemned as selfish. Any attempts at exploration of my thoughts, ideas, dreams or desires were squashed as meaningless and unimportant. No one was interested in what I thought or felt, or who I was, only in what I did –how I behaved.

Confidence is developed by doing something well. Therefore, it is based on what you do and how well you do it. Because of my core beliefs that I cannot depend on others and must do things for myself, also, that I am responsible for things getting done well, I have assumed responsibility for, and done a great many things from a very young age. I am competent and intelligent and have done most of those things successfully. Throughout life I have demonstrated competency in many varied areas. By comparing myself to others and receiving acknowledgment from them, I have gained confidence in my ability to do things well, perhaps better than most people. Thus I developed self-confidence from an early age.

Self-worth has nothing to do with achieving success large or small. It has nothing to do with doing anything. It only has to do with being who you are and feeling affirmed for that. It's a deep knowing that whatever you do or don't do, you will be accepted and valued just for being you.

It is developed when children are affirmed and accepted for who they are, regardless of how well they are able to perform. I was never affirmed or accepted for who I was and so I did not develop a sense of self-worth. Raised with harsh criticism and expectations often not age appropriate and impossible to meet, I became hounded by a feeling of worthlessness and spent many years trying to justify my right to exist.

The template for my identity had been clearly defined in childhood, and in adulthood, when I came to realize that it was a painful misfit, I was forced into a difficult choice. Honoring parental values was keeping me trapped forever in a world of tragic unreality, but rebelling and attempting to break out was running away, betraying what was good and noble, betraying "the cause," betraying those who suffered and died and opting for an "easy superficial" life. It took many years and the trauma of a near fatal accident before I was able to question that toxic belief.

Waking from the Nightmare

TWENTY-SIX

Searching for Meaning

WHEN I FINALLY ACKNOWLEDGED THAT THE PERSON I WAS raised to be was not who I was or wanted to be, I had to separate the many interwoven strands of my identity to discover which ones represented my true self and which were superimposed on me by others. It was not an easy task. I needed to discover who I really was before I could answer the question that had been troubling me for a long time: What was the purpose and meaning of my life?

The car accident was a watershed for me. It left me with a crushed foot, unable to walk and in constant pain. I also had a head injury, which severely affected my memory and concentration. I could not remember what had happened since the accident, but worse, I could not remember the names of my sisters, my address or phone number. My thinking was confused and I experienced *petit mal* seizures.

I forced myself back on my feet and three months later, afraid of losing my job if I stayed out much longer, I hobbled back to work on my crutches. I was working in Child Protective Services on an emergency response team but my physical disability prevented me from going out in the field. I was given a desk job, doing case quality review. This caused resentment on the part of my team-mates who now had to shoulder my share of the work. The atmosphere was stressful.

Very soon, it became clear that due to my brain injury, I could not perform the desk assignment, either. I lost my job. I was disabled.

Once again, everything was lost: my children, my home, my security and sense of self. Although I continued to have joint custody and see them during school vacations, my sons no longer lived with me and the loss was very painful. And, although it had been my decision to leave the marriage, as a result I no longer had a home of my own. Having lost my job, my financial security was in great jeopardy.

It was devastating. I had graduated from college at the age of nineteen, and since that time, except for a few short years after the children were born, I had always supported myself. I had always worked. I had a deep-seated subconscious belief that I had to take care of myself and that if I didn't, no one else would. I fell into a deep depression and for the next several months lived in a shadow world of darkness not knowing what my next steps would or could be. Unable to envision any future for myself, I was immobilized.

At first, much of the pain was dulled by the brain injury. For a long time, I barely knew who I was or what was happening. It is hard to describe the confused fog in which my life became enveloped. I was living in a dreamlike state, where reality and unreality were blended in a strange mix. In moments of clarity, faced with the enormity of my loss and the ruins of my life, I was devastated with grief and sank into a deep depression. This lasted for almost a year during which time some of my injuries were healing. Although in physical pain most of the time, despite the prediction of the orthopedist, I could finally walk without crutches and sometimes even without a cane.

The accident and its aftermath had physically, mentally and emotionally shattered me into pieces. It had changed my life in such profound ways, that emerging on the other side was a different person. The shattered pieces had to be re-assembled and the end result would never be the same. I could end up more crippled than before, more frightened, more dependent... *or* conversely I could emerge stronger, healthier finally autonomous and free. The healing would be a long, slow painful process. There was no silver bullet.

I was fortunate in a way that many others are not –I had a strong inner drive to heal. After many months, I woke up one morning to find that the sun was shining and life was beckoning. My depression was... gone. I had the sudden realization that my old life was finished and I had been reborn into a new one, one full of hope for the future. I struggled out of bed. The physical disability and pain were still there, but they would no longer immobilize me. I had a new life ahead of me and it was time to start living it.

I had left my first marriage about a year before the accident, and in the month prior to it had moved in with my new partner. We were both in the process of getting divorced and not ready to commit to another marriage. It took a couple more years before we took the plunge. By then, we had moved away from family, friends and our past to a beautiful but very isolated spot in the mountains of the north. I missed my children terribly, but having them for longer stretches of time during their school vacations provided more uninterrupted and quality time. My new husband was very much a loner. He wanted to work part time and write books, which he was able to do in our new environment.

My husband strongly believed in my intelligence and abilities, and he encouraged me to get more training and a grad-uate degree in psychotherapy and counseling. With his encouragement and support, I completed my graduate studies, got my degree and started a successful private practice. I enjoyed my work and got a lot of satisfaction from helping people. At the same time, I was constantly learning about how people are broken and how they can be helped to heal. I felt nurtured by my patients and by the work.

Once again, I was up for a challenge, I started to specialize in those difficult patients other therapists preferred to avoid and were happy to refer out. My focus became the Borderline Personality Disorder (BPD), which was also the topic of my thesis. The following quote from Mother Teresa, describes accurately the feelings of a person suffering from this condition. It also mirrored my own deepest feelings. She said:

" The greatest illness of today is not leprosy or tuberculosis, but rather the *experience of being unwanted, abandoned, betrayed.*"

These words were descriptive of my patients, but of me as well. I continued to desperately search for unconditional love, acceptance and security, as I continued to struggle with the demons of Fear, Depression and Despair. My troubled patients, struggling with the same demons, and learning from me how to overcome them became my teachers. It is so much easier to see, diagnose, treat and fix others than oneself. Which is, I came to believe, the reason why treating others in a loving way is so healing. I began to treat clients in a loving way.[1]

Doing therapy and helping others was a great gift to me and helped me on my own road to recovery. In understanding my patients, I started to understand myself. In helping them move from the suffering and pain to peace and contentment, I started to get a glimpse of the process and an idea of how it could be apply to my life.

Shortly after my second marriage, I became chronically ill with a mysterious ailment. My symptoms were vague: fatigue, weakness, no energy, complete lack of motivation. Negative tests led my doctors to suspect depression or hypochondria. But as the months went by, I lost an enormous amount of weight and became extremely debilitated. By four o'clock in the afternoon, I was counting the minutes until I could reasonably go to bed (usually 8 pm or so). Our social life was non-existent as I was non-functional well before evening. My husband diagnosed parasites,

but again tests proved negative. The doctors at that time believed and told us that there were no parasites in the North Country, where we resided. Finally, due to my deteriorating condition, I was hospitalized for several days of extensive testing. My small intestine was found to be so inflamed that I was unable to absorb any nutrients. Two specialists argued about the diagnosis: one said it was Crohn's Disease, the other was convinced it was ulcerative colitis. They both agreed my condition was critical and the prescription was for a lifetime on steroids. My husband was unconvinced and took me to a parasitologist in New York City.

I did not expect much by now. I knew something was very wrong with me, but the doctors couldn't agree on what it was and were dismissive of my vague complaints. This doctor was different. Before I could start listing my symptoms, he stopped me.

"Don't say anything, I'll tell you your symptoms."

And to my utter amazement, he rattled them all off, including those dismissed by previous doctors as irrelevant.

"Who told you?' I stammered.

"I've had parasites myself for thirty years, and I've been treating them in patients for almost as long. I can tell you are infected just by looking at you. Come. I'll show you."

He led me to an examination room and after taking a scraping off the wall of my intestine, carried the slide next door where a technician was sitting in front of a large microscope.

"You have two different kinds of parasites." I was told. "No wonder you've been so ill."

I looked at the strange stuff swimming under the microscope. Finally, someone had confirmed what was wrong with me and could fix it. He gave me lots of information, a prescription and most importantly: hope.

In one way, it was funny how this purely medical healing, fumbled by doctors over a period of many months, was achieved so easily by someone who knew the disease first-hand. His instantaneous recognition of my illness gave me confidence in him and made me feel validated. He made me feel whole even before I started the treatment.

After two days on the medication I started to feel better and eventually got my life back. And my hope for a better future came back.

Despite this, my private life was not happy. My husband and I shared many interests and values, but our cultural background was quite different causing endless irritation and conflict. To make things worse, we had diametrically differing personalities and needs. He needed a lot of time alone with his thoughts and creativity. I needed a lot of time together. He processed everything internally without the need or desire to discuss it until he had sorted it out within himself. I have an external process, meaning that I need to verbally bounce my thoughts off someone until I reach a resolution. This was extremely annoying for him, and frustrating for me.

My response to this dilemma was to keep reinventing myself in an effort to get his approval. When the "good wife" model didn't work I went back to school and became a professional in the hope of becoming his partner. But my husband was a lone ranger and partnership was not his style. Severely abused as a child, he had issues with women and trust, as well as difficulties with commitment. Every time we had a fight he would say he wanted a divorce and questioned why we were together. This triggered my fear of abandonment. He would say that he loved me but didn't like me. This was the same rejection I had experienced in my childhood. I was not accepted for who I was, and did not feel safe or loved.

I wanted to be consoled, understood and loved. Instead,

he told me I was too needy. That was, in fact, true. While it is normal to expect support, love and understanding in a relationship, anytime we need someone else to fill the black gaping hole within ourselves, we are expecting too much from another human being. No one can do this for us. Only we can do it for ourselves. But this was not a truth I was ready to hear and accept. The only way I could deal with the pain of what felt like another rejection was to lose myself in my work. I studied more, worked harder and became a better therapist. I studied marriage therapy in an effort to better understand our problems and heal our marriage, and became very good at that. I helped many couples through their difficulties, but was unable to improve our marriage in any significant way. Living far away from any community where I could make friends, I felt very alone. The poems I wrote during those years describe the grief, loneliness and despair I felt.

Loneliness
Between two narrow boulders
I glimpsed the distant horizon
An ocean of space
Endless infinity
Emptiness that even my love
cannot fill.

Death
If I should die tonight,
Let me go gently, gladly toward the light.
Let no tears for things undone
Or people left behind
Disturb the rest and peace of weary heart and
    mind.

I Talked to My Companions
I talked to my companions

Anger and despair.
Nothing new to report.
So I take an aspirin
And curl up with the pain
Waiting for it to dull.
Then I will distract myself with work.
That is life.

Another painful shock was awaiting me. After my mother's death, my Dad married a woman from Poland and returned to live out his old age in his homeland. After a few years, I went to visit him in the city of my birth. For years I had lived in exile, and now, filled with excitement and joy, I was going back home to the city of legend and heroism, back home to my country.

Unfortunately for me, the country I arrived in bore no resemblance to the one I had known and loved from my childhood. The pre-War Poland, in the shadow of which I had grown up, was dead and gone. Everything was changed, most of all the people. During and after the Warsaw uprising, and during the ensuing Soviet occupation the majority of the original residents of Warsaw had been killed or deported and were replaced by an influx of people from villages, hamlets and rural communities with their own cultural background much different from that of the original city residents. Not only that, everyone had been affected and transformed by forty years of Communism. Except for the language, there was nothing familiar to me about the new Poland. To my amazement and dismay, while I was there, I felt more American than Polish.

Again, as always, I was different. I did not belong. This was not the homeland I had dreamed about my whole life. This was not home. The pre-War Polish culture, in which I was raised, no longer existed. I had spent years of my childhood and youth nostalgic and longing for a homeland that did not exist and never would. There were millions of exiles, who experienced the same loss. And yet, as a Polish writer so poignantly expressed the feelings of my broken heart:

> *"Three years in a row I plowed the land and sowed the seed. But I had no harvest. Strange, how history can't come up with a new joke.*
>
> *Two truths had their day of reckoning. For the frontier this is not the first time. The forests continue to moan in the wind as they have done for years, tree sap flows on the moors, the earth gives off its fragrance, the river glistens, ants in the forest have built back their hills in the clearings chopped out by the war, and are weaving along their paths of pine needles.*
>
> *It is not the first time for this land, not the first time in the memory of the frontier, nor the first time for God in heaven, nor for the wise order of the world, nor for Eternal Wisdom and Eternal Goodness which like the ray of sun permeate the world, causing every particle to grow better - so that the world grows better all the time. But what of it all -when for the broken human heart, it's always the first time. "*

Melchior Wankowicz, Na Tropach Smetka

When I returned to the United States, I discovered that not being a Pole did not magically make me an American. Here, too, I was a stranger. This realization left me more bereft than ever. Now, I became a "person without a country". It was the painful cutting loose of the final tie to the unreality of my past. I was now free to look ahead and move into a new future. In time, it freed me from my feeling of obligation. I no longer felt guilty for being unable to serve my homeland in any meaningful way. I was finally able to accept that while Poland was the country of my birth, it was no longer my country. This realization provided closure and healing for my broken heart. It allowed me to start moving on.

The lessons, I painfully learned, apply to anyone who discovers at some point in their life that the path they were on perhaps from childhood, is not the true path for them, and decides to abandon it. Those, for example, raised in religious fundamentalism, who choose a more moderate way or worse a completely different religion, or no religion at all, are often renounced, ostracized and bullied by family and friends. They are literally told they are going to hell –to eternal damnation. People living in societies or families with any strong dogma, that is part of a family or group identity and as such is not open to being questioned, face similar rejection, condemnation and punishment. It could be a religious or political affiliation, or it could be the prevalent social structure. Questioning common attitudes, values or way of life is always emotionally dangerous, and sometimes physically so.

My health problems were not over. For many years, I struggled with mild seizures due to the head injury sustained during my car accident. Usually, these were no more than brief blackouts followed by a period of confusion. But at times of stress, they became much more unpleasant. I

had written in my journal describing my experience.

Before the episode for several hours, it feels like a Doomsday cloud is descending on me –dark, heavy, menacing. I tense up becoming more rigid than ever, hyper-vigilant, irritable. Everything is noticed and anything that is not quite right bothers me. I am super-sensitized and over-reactive. Very vulnerable and defended. Very brittle. I need verbal reassurance and space.

The cloud envelops me and I am devastated: emotionally raw and depressed, physically unable to function. Distortions blur my vision. My balance and spatial sense are off, brain is foggy, I am completely confused. Unable to think or make any decisions. Completely on the edge of a precipice, any smallest stress pushes me over. Feeling helpless like a small child who needs care. Extremely sensitive and vulnerable to harsh words or any kind of pressure. Out of control physically and emotionally. Very confused and frightened. Want to cry or just disappear. Ashamed at loss of control.

Afterwards, I'm extremely tired, need rest and sleep. Need quiet, loving reassurance and calm. I crave warmth, love, caring, patience. Need lots of sleep for several days, ten to twelve hours a night. If there is not enough rest, warmth, acceptance, I get tense and collapse into physical illness. More shame at failure of self-control.

Despite these setbacks, I struggled on. For some reason, quitting was never an option, and since I assumed responsibility for my life, it was up to me to get things right. I was a fighter and surrender was not something I did. I continued trying to decipher the purpose of my suffering and the meaning and purpose of my life. I slogged on.

TWENTY-SEVEN

The Hero's Journey

LIFE IS A JOURNEY. WE LEAVE HOME AND EMBARK ON A PERIOD of transition, which in the end, if we follow the correct path, will bring us to the goal of our journey: the destination. In the normal course of child development, an adolescent grows into young adulthood and is eager to leave home and strike out on his/her own journey traveling their own unique path to their own destination. The journey is always dangerous and filled with traps that can ensnare the unprepared. It is a rite of passage. It is the way a human child grows and matures into a self-sufficient adult. In mythology, it is the Hero's journey.

Home is always the point of departure. As we embark on the journey, we leave behind the comfort and security of family, relationships and the familiar. Home represents the safety of the womb, childhood memories, and belonging, or the place we have consciously chosen to set down roots. As someone said: "Home is the place where when you return, they have to take you in." Once we have left for good, we are on our own in a dangerous world.

A fledgling bird exercises its wings until they are strong enough for it to leave the safety of the nest. Sometimes, there is accident and the little bird falls out of the nest before being able to fly. It is then completely vulnerable to predators and its survival is at great risk. While leaving the nest is always scary, being thrust out prematurely is traumatic. I had been thrust out of the nest twice in my early childhood, and then in my first marriage was not able to construct a secure one that would hold, nurture and protect me. So, I jumped out fearing its imminent collapse.

But despite the heartache and many difficulties, I was not jumping out of my second marriage. I had come to understand: that too would be running away, and whatever problems I had brought to my current relationship I would be taking with me into any future ones. I knew I had to struggle, persevere and not give up if there was to be a chance at finding stability, peace and some measure of happiness. So, I continued to struggle -- with myself, with my husband, with our marriage.

There is no doubt that by my mid years I had been away from home for a long time, which means I was in the transit stage of my journey. This stage is characterized by impermanence. It is a temporary state of flux and change, constant movement, entailing feelings of loss, insecurity, being a stranger and not belonging. It is a time of exploration, always involving danger, trial and error. It can be an exciting time or a very difficult. As you can see from my story, for me it was very hard.

Destination is the ultimate goal, which we struggle so hard to achieve and which gives meaning and purpose to the journey. For most of us, arrival comes late in life. But there are signposts, which if we learn to recognize provide guidance and encouragement.

After my husband retired from his practice, he started to travel extensively teaching workshops and seminars all over the world. I continued my practice for two more years, feeling envious of his tours to exciting places. I too, wanted a chance to travel. Eventually, I closed my practice and accompanied him on his tours. Always the business manager in our relationship, I helped organize his workshops and took care of all the mundane aspects of life and business so that he could focus without interruption on his creative and original work. I deeply admired that aspect of him, especially as I felt I had no creative abilities at all.

My husband tried hard to encourage me. He believed I was an exceptionally good therapist and should continue my career along those lines, as well as try my hand at writing. But fear stood in the way. Pursuing my career would mean that I would not be with him most of the time and that raised the specter of abandonment. If I wasn't there to take care of everything and manage his life, he might discover that he didn't need me. In fact, he might discover that he didn't want me. I would be left alone and I couldn't face that possibility.

Subconsciously, I was still a slave to the perfectionism of my father, whose motto was: anything you don't do well (read perfectly) is not worth doing. Trying something new always entails the risk of mistakes. Theodore Roosevelt once said: "The only man who never makes mistakes is the man who never does anything." Since to me a mistake signified failure, and failure was not an option, I did nothing I could not do well; I could not try something new. I was paralyzed by my fear of not being perfect, of failing, once again my father's test.

During this time, a potent experience unblocked the logjam of perfectionism and fear. Undoubtedly, some will consider this experience highly unusual... but for me it changed everything.

I continued to accompany my husband on his travels and take care of the more tedious and routine aspects of our life. Mostly, it was a lot of fun and I enjoyed it a lot. In time, I noticed that a number of his students both on the East and West coast of the United States were followers of a spiritual master I had never heard of prior to this time. His name was

Meher Baba. Both my husband and I were distinctly averse to gurus, but we were amazed and impressed by the caliber of people who were his followers. We had known, liked and respected them for years before finding out about their connection to Baba. They did not wear robes, chant or advertise their beliefs. They were definitely not weird in any way. In fact, most were very well put together and quite successful in their chosen professions.

We decided to find out more, were loaned and read a short book about the life and work of Meher Baba, who was of Persian origin, but had been born and died in India. I was mildly intrigued and purchased the memoirs of his chief disciple. That book shocked me to the core.

I could not understand how anyone, considered a spiritual guide, could act or treat others the way He did. Meher Baba, I decided, was a controlling tyrant, mentally unbalanced and given to outbursts of violence. I was completely disgusted and knew that this was not for me. It was puzzling how intelligent, educated people could accept such treatment and continue for a lifetime in his service. For me, it was inconceivable. I thought that was the end of my involvement with what seemed like a strange cult of personality by people who otherwise seemed completely normal.

About six months later, we went to visit one of my husband's students. Jason had just moved his family to a tiny town in northern California, where he established his practice of acupuncture. Jason comes the closest to a highly spiritually evolved being that I know. In religious language, I would say he has the qualities of holiness that are rarely encountered. He and his wife are followers of Meher Baba and travel regularly to Baba's ashram in India spending time with the elderly disciples who are still alive. At the time of our visit, Jason had just returned from one such pilgrimage and brought back at the request of a friend a large painted portrait of Baba's head and shoulders.

This painting was standing by the entrance waiting to be picked up. As I started walking by to get inside, I glanced at the face and was riveted in place by the eyes. I couldn't move. I was transfixed. Like a bolt of lightening, the recognition hit me that this was the face of Christ, come again into the world for our sake, for my sake. As his eyes bored into my heart, I knew without any doubt that He had come to claim me and that henceforth I would always be His. The sense of Light and Love pouring into me completely filled and obliterated the black hole that had always been at the center of my being. I had never experienced such ecstasy. Tears of joy were flowing down my face and I just stood there as if in a trance, oblivious of everyone and everything around me. The tears washed away all the grief and loss; all the pain was being healed. I felt infused with Light and Love.

Finally, I came to my senses and apologized to our hosts for the flood -- but the tears periodically started to flow again. Fortunately, they understood completely, as they too at some point had experienced something similar. Many years later, someone said it was a conversion experience, and it did, in fact, feel a lot like what St. Paul described as his encounter with Christ at the gates of Damascus. Like for Paul, this event was life changing for me.

Healing the Pain

TWENTY-EIGHT

Finding Love

For the first time I felt fully the unconditional love and the acceptance of me as I was, that I had always craved. The insecurity and fear were banished by the realization that this Love was eternal, it would be there with me forever. There could be no question of abandonment. Baba took up residence in my heart. His presence filled the emptiness and cast out the dark. The black hole was no more and I felt whole. I later read that He used to say it is His habit to sleep in men's hearts, it is up to us to wake Him. Somehow He woke up with a bang in my heart, and has been there ever since that time.

It was not only my outer life that was changed, I, too, was a different person, ready to face life in a different way. He said that He did not come to teach, that mankind had been given enough teachings and all they had to do was to live by them. His mission was different. He came to open human hearts and he certainly smashed mine open. I came to see how in the constant effort to protect myself, I had been erecting barriers to keep others out. My heart was closed for most of my life, as I tried to create small islands of safety for me, and those close to me. Mother Teresa had said: "The problem with the world is that we draw the circle of our family too small." I was certainly guilty of that. Now I started to understand the concept of inclusivity, of radical hospitality. My heart was opening to others, and I found it difficult now to keep anyone out. There was an exponential increase in the circle of my family and loved ones. The idea that we are all one was starting to make sense. In *The Way of St. Francis*, Murray Bodo wrote:

> *"The exclusive love of anyone or anything is essentially isolation and leads to loneliness. Only a love that is inclusive of everything God has made can make me whole, and to the extent that I can belong to the universe without trying to cling possessively to anything in it, to that extent I am freed of loneliness."*

I started to understand why I no longer felt lonely and isolated. I now felt a part of a large community: one to which every human being belonged. And, in a larger evolutionary sense, all of creation was a part of the greater unity to which I belonged. I would never again be a stranger.

From a spiritual standpoint, many people believe that there is within each one of us a place where the divine dwells and which is the home and safe place of our soul. Finding our way back to this place is the journey.

Of course, not everyone sees life through a spiritual prism. There are certainly other valid ways of perceiving the world, understanding our life and its trajectory. Poet Robert Bly, and mythologist, Joseph Campbell, talk about "following your bliss". Professor of psychology and education, Mihaly Csikszentmihalyi has written about finding "Flow" as a way of enhancing creativity and quality of life. Psychiatrist, Carl Jung, as well as psychologists in the tradition of humanistic psychology, such as James Hillman and many others, consider finding one's "True Self" as the key to finding oneself and inner peace. It may all be the same. Regardless of what we call it, we must establish some ground of inner being that gives us a stable foundation on which to build our lives.

My universe continued to expand. I had always been a very cerebral person. Highly intelligent, and trained from childhood that emotions will get me nowhere whereas a good rational argument will, I valued logic and reason above feelings and intuition. Because of the emotional trauma experienced in childhood, I was for many years completely cut off from my feelings. My intuition was undeveloped and I had no faith in it. Since the shattering of my heart by Baba, I started reconnecting with feelings and my intuition opened up. This allowed me a completely different and broader view of reality. It was as if all my life until then I had been suffering from tunnel vision. Suddenly, I saw the world in multiple dimensions I had not known even existed.

Baba became a constant presence in my heart and a constant companion in my daily life. I would talk to him as to a close trusted friend and advisor. When overwhelmed or distressed, I would just call to Him: "Help me, Baba, I can't do this by myself. Help me." He always does. He does not ask for much, just to remember him all the time, and if that is too hard, at least four times a day. It's easy to remember him when I wake up and go to sleep, and I use my computer and iPod to remind me during the day.

The proof of change is in change itself.

About two years after these events, I was once again accompanying my husband to a seminar he was teaching twice a year in Florida. While there, the Director of the acupuncture school that had been hosting his seminars approached us with the sad news that the school would be closing shortly. An appeal was made to us to save the school. Two other persons would partner with us if only my husband would agree to lend his name and we would put up a third of the capital needed to keep the school running until it could get back on its feet. There was an administration and faculty in place. We would not be called upon for more than attend one or two annual Board meetings. We had to regretfully refuse. Running a school did not fit into our life plan. We had no knowledge, experience or interest. Already, older and retired, we were contemplating a quiet life with, perhaps, a bit of travel. Financially, we were comfortable, but not by any means wealthy and such an investment would stretch our means. We both agreed, we could not do it.

Driving north, we stopped as usual for a few days at the Meher Baba Retreat Center in South Carolina. On the second day, my husband asked me if I was getting a message from Baba. I told him I was, and not one I was happy to hear. We both strongly felt that Baba wanted us to go back and get involved in the school. It was a clear calling, and we didn't debate it. We turned around, drove back to Florida and embarked on our assigned task.

It proved much harder and more costly in every way, than we had been led to believe. Instead of the initial investment we were asked to make, it soon became clear that in order to survive, the school would need to be propped up for a number of years. Instead of running smoothly, the old staff needed to be replaced. Since they were operating on a shoestring, there was no money for a competent new Director, and I volunteered take on the full-time job. This entailed a move to Florida, where we lived and worked for the next eight years. During my tenure the school had become a state licensed and accredited college, with an excellent reputation in the field for its academic program. Upon my retirement, we were able to hire a director with experience in higher education. The college was on its way to a successful future.

I could have never accomplished this task without the changes wrought in my life and personality following my encounter with Baba. When faced with putting about a third of our retirement savings into a most uncertain investment, my husband, who is almost twenty years older than I, told me this was my retirement money that we would be risking and perhaps losing. He asked me to decide. I felt we had been giving our marching orders by Baba and did not hesitate. I have been called parsimonious. I like to save. In the past, my insecurity would not have allowed me to put money into a risky venture, and I am still highly risk averse but as soon as I felt sure this was Baba's plan I had no second thoughts.

Fear of failure was another driving force within me that fell by the wayside. This freed me in many ways from the ties that bound me in the past. I had had absolutely no experience with running any school, much less an institution of higher learning. As the new director, I needed to gain accreditation for the school, no easy task. Then I had to get the state to license us as a college: another formidable undertaking. Finally, I had to juggle money to keep us afloat. A part of this entailed raising funds. Asking for money was very difficult for me, but it had to be done and it was my job to do it. Also, I had had no experience with accounting, and when I presented my first budget to the Advisory Board, the chairman, a professional accountant, looked puzzled. "This is not a budget," he informed me. Embarrassed, I bought a book on the subject, redid and resubmitted something that professionals could recognize and accept as a budget.

While the end results were satisfactory, I made lots of mistakes along the way and could not always delay action while trying to make it perfect. There were two fundamental shifts in my internal beliefs that allowed me to do this difficult work of nurturing and growing the school.

The first change was that, I no longer assumed responsibility for the end result. All I felt responsible for was doing the very best I could. This I could control. The outcome was not up to me, as my power and control were limited. I felt like an officer in battle who having received orders from the general is responsible for executing them to the best of his ability. He is only responsible for his assignment and his actions. He is not in charge of the whole battle and not responsible for its final outcome. This new belief freed me from worry about the end result, and allowed me to focus on doing the job.

The second shift entailed the understanding and acceptance that as I myself was an imperfect being nothing I did would be perfect. I finally realized that perfection was not required, and that doing my best was good enough. Although it had not been enough for my Father, it was enough for the God who made me imperfect as I was and who did not require more than my best.

Most of my life, I was paralyzed by the fear that my efforts would not be good enough. This fear held me back from new experiences and blocked completely my creativity. My new understanding freed me to act and to take risks. If what I did wasn't perfect (like the completely inadequate budget I submitted, which was the subject of many chuckles over the years), I did not feel devastated —I knew I had to do better and that I would have another chance. In the end, I became very good at preparing budgets!

Another apprehension that ruled my life was the fear of abandonment and the subsequent terror of being alone. I have already described the panic attacks that plagued me since early childhood and did not go away in adulthood. I had always made sure, as much as possible, to not be alone. This fear probably played a large role in my giving up my practice when my husband retired and started extensive travel. It was a huge obstacle to my freedom, and limited the choices I could make. When I became the full time director of the school I could only take a very limited amount of time off, and my husband wanted to be in his beloved mountains up North. While, very involved with the College, he was able to take the summers off, while I was not. We lived in a small cottage and I resented being left alone for months. But, in time, I came to see how it was another blessing for me. I found that my panic attacks were gone. It's not that I no longer felt any fear. It's that fear no longer ruled my life. I knew deep within that whatever trials God had in mind for me, He would give me the strength to bear the. I would never again be alone.

The results of all these profound changes are continuing to unfold in my life, as I tread new ground venturing into new territory. One result of these changes is my ability to write this book. It exemplifies the sort of risk I could not have taken before. Another example is my choice, after retiring from my position at the College, to spend my winters in beautiful Sarasota, near my son and six grandchildren. For several years, my husband continued teaching and working with faculty at the College, two hundred miles away. So, I have been living alone for several months every year, enjoying the time I could finally devote to my family. This was a choice I could not have made before liberation from the bonds of fear.

My life has been a long, long journey, not just in miles travelled and in years lived, but from being lost and in bondage to trauma and others' demands and expectations... to inner freedom to love, accept and be my true self. My new freedom allows me to continue to explore the many exciting possibilities life has on offer. Life in my old age is better than ever before.

I realize how my story has been told through the prism of my very personal experience, which will not resonate with all readers. I cannot write about the Truth. I can only write about my experience, my thoughts, my beliefs. I can only write about my truth as I see it. This means that while all the facts reported in this book are, to the best of my knowledge accurate, their interpretation and meaning is completely subjective.

As a psychotherapist, trained to analyze life and human problems through the lens of psychology, I have given much thought to understanding and explaining my life and transformation using a scientific rather than a spiritual perspective. In the last part of this book, I would like to offer that alternate explanation for those interested in psychology and those for whom the healing and transformation as I recounted it is not convincing, but who are curious as to how such a transformations can and do occur.

TWENTY-NINE

Emergence

"Most people have, at some time or another, to stand alone and to suffer, and their final shape is determined by their response to their probation: they emerge either the slaves of circumstance, or in some sense captains of their soul." Charles E. Raven, "A Wanderer's Way"

LIKE MOST PEOPLE I WANTED TO BE HAPPY, AND LIKE FOR MOST people for me that meant love, security and a sense of belonging, a family, a home. My early life and adolescence left me without those elements of security and happiness, and I spent many years of my life sad, frightened, depressed and unhappy. But I was always a fighter and giving up was not an option. I took responsibility for my life. Blaming others for my problems or situation did not occur to me, if anyone was to blame it was myself. I was the captain of my ship, if not yet my soul. So, I struggled on with my demons, always trying to change myself for the better in the hope of creating a future happier than my past. One of the hardest issues for me was the terrible cruelty and injustice to which I had been exposed as a witness from childhood: the cause of so much suffering and death. I was raised to remember, and while the memory triggered painful reactions, I felt it my duty to never forget. I hated with a passion the Germans, who had inflicted such atrocities on my people. I could never forget or forgive. And yet, the hatred kept me in chains. It did not lead to healing.

Reading *The Once and Future King*, an Arthurian novel by T. H. White, I was mesmerized by this passage:

Man must be ready to say: Yes, since Cain there has been injustice, but we can only set the misery right if we accept a status quo. Lands have been robbed, men slain, nations humiliated. Let us now start afresh without remembrance, rather than live forward and backward at the same time. We cannot build the future by avenging the past. Let us sit down as brothers and accept the Peace of God.

This spoke directly to my experience, my past, my trauma. It offered a new and radically different perspective on how to move into the future. The quote profoundly moved and affected me, but I could not consent to its meaning. It talked about accepting the unacceptable, about forgetting, about letting go. Sitting down as brothers implied forgiveness. No, I was not ready for this, and would not be for a very long time.

I think the biggest factor in my healing was embracing an active role in life. Taking responsibility for my life made me a survivor not a victim. That is a key point. The victim is helpless. The survivor has power. I have found in my practice, that every time a patient was focused on what was being done to him/her thus assuming the posture of a victim, unless I was able to turn that around and get them to assume responsibility, to embrace their power, no forward movement was possible. Victims are acted upon. They cannot act. They have no choice but to accept what happens to them. Survivors can act in different ways, sometimes they can't survive physically, but at least psychologically they can resist. They can fight back. They have choices and don't have to accept passively their fate. Being or becoming a fighter, by taking responsibility for your life is the first crucial step in any healing, especially from trauma.

By taking responsibility I don't mean blaming yourself for the acts of others. We all bear responsibility for our actions. Two professional women get mugged and raped while walking a dark city street. One is plunged into darkest depression, gives up her job, living a diminished life of fear, keeping suicidal thoughts at bay through massive medication and struggling to get by on disability. The other, enraged by the violence, turns her energies into organizing a movement against rape, educating the public and helping other women avoid the horrific trauma she suffered. Neither woman is responsible for what happened to her. But they are both responsible for what they do with their life after the fact. While the first woman becomes a victim defeated by the assault, the second becomes an activist transforming it into something positive for others. In doing so, she transcends her own pain allowing healing to begin.

Please understand, I am not blaming the "victim" who, unable to pick herself up and move on, ended in a sad downward spiral. Perhaps she was truly unable to actively engage in a healing process due to a complete lack of resources. Excluding those with exceptional inner strength and resilience, we all need help and support in times of crisis. Traumatic events are always destabilizing and we must have enough stability in other areas of life to overcome their destructive effects. Stable and loving relationships, a network of friends and family, adequate income to meet basic needs, good mental and physical health, and access to therapy or psychologically sensitive teachers are all important factors in healing. Missing any of these critical elements makes recovery more difficult. Missing many makes it all but impossible.

THIRTY

Facing the Pain

FACING SUFFERING IS A COMPLICATED THING AND ONE CAN ERR on the side of passivity, as in the previous illustration, and also by the wrong sort of action. In order to heal, we must face the pain, and yet we must do it in the correct way.

As David Ford says in *The Shape of Living*: *"Assent to suffering is a knife-edge. On one side are the wrong sorts of passivity that give in to evil, fail to value life and health, and glorify suffering as something good in itself. On the other side are the wrong sorts of activity that make elimination of suffering an absolute, strive above all for comfort and control, and fail to see the superficiality and boredom of a world without risk of things going wrong. In between is the apprenticeship that can only be served with those who know the trade of suffering and have learned when and how to accept it and assent to it.*

They recognize that great suffering is overwhelming and has therefore simply to be undergone. There comes appoint when the questions change. Then we no longer ask about how to avoid a particular suffering or even why it is happening to us. Instead, all our resources are focused on how we might come through it, and our ultimate question becomes (if we can learn from those who know the trade best): What is it for? The basic trust is that suffering, evil, and even death do not have the last word about life...
"

I was fortunate on several counts. Despite my PTSD, I always had much inner strength and resilience. I always had adequate though sometimes minimal resources to meet my basic needs. From time to time I had access to therapy, and always in my life I had people who in their own way loved me, cared about me and were there for the long haul. They were all my teachers.

First came my parents who instilled in me life long values: truth and justice. They ingrained in me the belief that life has a higher purpose than fulfillment of self-centered desires. They introduced me to the concept of service to others and dedication to a cause beyond my own immediate gain. They also set the foundations of my character by setting high ethical standards: integrity, loyalty, honor.

My first husband uncritically accepted and loved me for who I appeared to be, or, as I was at the time of our marriage. This filled a deep longing within me. The price of his love was that I would stay eternally in my gilded cage. I was accepted and loved as I was, though I could not grow and change. His uncritical love and acceptance was a great gift, which made me feel secure and like a ray of sunshine stimulated growth.

My second husband gave me no security. His love was very conditioned on my behavior, which he did not like for the most part. He was always ready to bail out of the marriage. What he did give me was recognition and admiration of my potential and the encouragement and support for my growth. He envisioned what I could become and inspired me to pursue my mental, psychological and spiritual development. He modeled for me the ability to persevere, to work hard, taught me how to build a foundation. Despite his criticism, in his own way he always loved me. When I studied Imago marriage therapy, I understood what it was that bound us so tightly together so that despite the rocky road we were travelling we remained committed to each other for complicated psychological reasons. Neither of us was capable of real love, but we were both struggling to learn.

As babies and toddlers, my children were the only people, except for my nanny, to give me unconditional love. I loved them back with all my heart. Their love nurtured and sustained me healing some of the negative beliefs I had developed: especially, the one that I was unlovable. Without them and their love, I could not have become who I am. Later, they gave me a more painful but no less valuable gift. They were both very hurt by my leaving the family and it took many years for them to forgive. During those years, they repeatedly shattered my heart into pieces with what felt like sledge-hammer blows.

Many times, when my older son was struggling I wanted desperately to help, but all my offers were rejected.

"Why won't you let me help you?" I pleaded over and over again.

"When I was growing up and needed help, no one was there for me. Now I don't need anyone, I can do it on my own." Was his consistent response.

There is nothing more painful for a mother watching her child struggling and refusing her help. It made me feel I was a complete failure as a mother. Nor, could I help my grandchildren. When my sons struggled raising their offspring, I learned early and painfully that my suggestions were not wanted. I was informed that having been absent for their childhood years, I was not a fit grandmother.

Over the years, I came to feel that having abandoned him, I was the cause of all my younger son's problems and unhappiness. I felt responsible for his pain. He would recount in great detail the misery he had suffered growing up with a father and brother who bonded against him. Not sharing their interest in sports and fishing, he loved music and art, which they, in turn, did not value. Thus he felt alienated, misunderstood and unappreciated – much as I had felt growing up.

Although he was willing to accept any help I could give, it always felt like it was always too little, too late. Nothing I could do would ever make up the damage I had done to him by leaving.

Since I loved my sons beyond measure, it broke my heart to know that one needed help but would not accept it from me, while the other one I could never help enough. And worse, that all the pain they now suffered was attributable to choices I had made. This realization and caused me great sorrow.

Just as the car accident painfully jolted me out of my old life and catapulted me into the future, these excruciatingly painful blows were necessary to open up the heart rendered hard and closed by trauma, and encrusted with defenses I had built up over time. My heart desperately needed to be cracked open and my sons' pain and anger helped do it. Without that, I could not have taken the next step on my journey of healing.

THIRTY-ONE

Understanding and Empathy

MY PATIENTS WERE ALL MY TEACHERS. THEY TAUGHT ME empathy and understanding, patience and sensitivity. I learned from them that I could not fix every problem by employing good techniques, by doing: that sometimes it took just sitting with someone, just being there for them, just witnessing their pain until they were ready to move on. Some of them demonstrated examples of good people doing bad things. Understanding where they were coming from, I could not be critical and judgmental. The trust my patients showed me by opening up their hearts and minds and sharing with me their wounded-ness, that part each of us tries to cover up and hide, taught me about a different kind of courage. Being invited to enter their hearts and minds in such an intimate way taught me about a different kind of love, *agape*. I could not help loving every one of them. My own heart, heretofore restricted to loving family and close friends, was now opening to the *'other'*. My ability to accept, respect and appreciate differences grew.

The above example of the two women who were raped, is very black and white demonstrating one person disengaging from life as a result of trauma (drugs, mental illness), and the other engaging with a cause. In this example, disengagement becomes negative while engagement has a positive outcome. Reality is far more complicated. The actual point here is not the path of engagement or its opposite, but rather the stance one assumes as someone with decision-making power, or someone who relinquishes control over his/her life and fate. When one is very ill, disengagement can be the best healing strategy. Running around further debilitates the organism while withdrawal into inactivity and rest promotes its ability to heal. Disengagement can be an active choice rather than a passive surrender.

Both strategies of engagement and disengagement can play a positive or negative role in life. Both active and passive strategies can be useful on a short-term basis. It is when we give up the active pursuit of our goals and resign ourselves to accepting what others or life dish out, that we give up our ability to move forward. We are no longer captains of our ship, just helpless passengers along for the ride to a destination of someone else's choice. So the question here is not whether we choose to be active or passive in a given situation, it is whether we choose at all.

For me, not choosing was not an option. It would mean giving up my individuality and freedom. Even when I chose to do what others expected, rather than what I wanted (going to Scout Jamboree), it was my choice. I suppose that was why I was considered a rebel, a non-conformist, different. But being a non-conformist is not the only path to freedom. My adored sister, Helen, was completely different from me. In childhood, her wishes coincided for the most part with those of our parents, and so she chose to do what was expected thus earning praise instead of the criticism and punishment that was my lot. So again, the question is not what choices one makes, strategies one employs or path one travels, it's assuming responsibility for the choices one makes that matters. This is what empowers us to steer our own course.

As I've described in detail, I felt empowered to make decisions, I felt I had choices. They were not always good decisions, in fact many of them were terrible mistakes with painful consequences for me and my loved ones. Here again, the critical issue was taking responsibility. Through the dark periods of my life, empathetic friends would sometimes tell me that I tend to always blame myself, that everything is not my fault. But I instinctively understood that by blaming another person and avoiding responsibility, I would be giving up my power to influence and change my future. We can only change ourselves. But as a critical ingredient in every equation, when we change ourselves we automatically change the result/outcome.

Finding myself as a young adult miserably unhappy and frightened, I took action. I married an older man, who I thought would protect me from the goblins, I distanced myself from my family of origin which was connected so strongly to the roots of my misery, I distracted myself by becoming heavily engaged in good works (social justice, environment) and I continued to educate myself through reading and therapy. Driven by fear, and in a desperate attempt to find purpose and meaning in my painful life I kept running at a frantic pace.

When my marriage did not provide the support and understanding I desperately needed, I abandoned it deeply wounding my husband and children. I felt driven to move on to keep running, away from my demons and in the search of the ineffable Grail. It was years later that I ran across the profound thinker, Christopher Bryant, who wrote in *The River Within*:

"A person does not realize himself at the expense of others."

But that was many years later. At the time I acted reactively in response to my inner drives, insensitive and oblivious to the price others were paying for my lack of conscious awareness.

Our ancient brain is programmed for survival. Running from danger is a common and frequently effective strategy, which I utilized to the hilt. The problem is that while it can get you away from danger thus ensuring survival, it does nothing to advance you on your journey nor does it bring you closer to your goal. Of course, survival must come first even if it involves running in circles instead of advancing. Without survival there is no reaching life's goal.

Unfortunately, PTSD distorts the brain's neurological circuits. Like the auto-immune diseases, which identify normal cells incorrectly as enemy intruders and attack them causing inflammation and other serious problems, the PTSD brain triggers constant danger alarms when there is no actual threat. Like most people suffering with this disorder, I kept running in circles for most of my life, trying to escape non-existent danger, just trying to survive.

There are a number of unfortunate results of always operating in survival mode. The ancient part of the brain has three basic drives, and while survival is paramount the others have to do with the quality of life. One is the drive to experience enjoyment – like the lizard sunning itself on a warm rock, the other is the drive to express aliveness through sex and play. While the brain is pre-occupied with survival, the other two are relegated to a back seat. So, one of the side effects of my constant pumping adrenaline in an effort to escape annihilation was my inability to fully enjoy the pleasures of life. One has to stop running and feel safe before one can relax and enjoy pleasurable sensations or abandon oneself to great sex. I could not stop.

In a journal, I once wrote:

"At the center of my existence, in a place I am always very reluctant to visit, there is a deep dark lake of sorrow, despair, anguish, pain, loss".

The truth is that it was not a matter of *visiting* that place. It was a matter of life and death for me to avoid it. That place was like a black hole in the fabric of my being which threatened to swallow me whole and destroy me. I had to avoid it at all cost. I had to keep running.

At first, I was the "perfect" wife and mother. I cooked from scratch, baked bread and sewed clothes for the family. It was quite a feat, as I had acquired none of these skills growing up and had to learn them on my own, through reading and through trial and error. It was a challenge, which kept me distracted for a few years. During this time, I was immensely nurtured by my young sons, who were the joy of my life. In a letter many years later, I wrote:

> *"The birth of my children was the greatest joy I ever experienced. I had never felt such happiness before they came into my life. I have never loved anyone in the way or with the intensity that I loved them. While this may be true for other parents, my feelings were magnified by the fact that I had never experienced that kind of joy before or since."*

Concerned about the fact that my husband hated his job, I encouraged him to switch to social work in which I knew he would excel, and which, I thought, he would find rewarding. It meant a fifty percent cut in pay. I was not worried. Happiness and fulfillment meant to me more than money. I had previously encouraged him to buy a thirty-foot boat as fishing and the ocean were his passion. I wanted him to be happy as if in his contentment, I too would find mine. When he switched jobs, we could no longer afford the boat, but I thought he would consent to chartering once or twice a month to pay the expenses. He tried and hated it. He was a loner, and could not tolerate 'fools' who didn't know anything about fishing or boating. Money became very tight and I returned to work full time.

Now I started running faster than ever. Although I no

longer cooked from scratch or baked bread or sewed our clothes, I did have a full time job, two young children, who needed my time and attention and a household to manage. My husband came from the generation where men did not pitch in to cook, do laundry or cleaning. Given my background, I would have felt like a failure if I couldn't manage by myself.

As my marriage continued to deteriorate, I escaped home by engaging in ever more time consuming activities. These were not recreational in nature. They were always good causes in the service of others. I was always fighting evil in the service of justice. This allowed me to feel that I was sacrificing my time, energy and life to a higher purpose, and avoid acknowledging how I was escaping my real responsibilities.

My second marriage played out in a different way. Like my first husband, my second one was a loner. He was also a writer, who required many hours a day to think and write. Writing is a solitary occupation, and I was frustrated by the lack of time he had for me and the fact that like my first husband he was not a communicator. His process was internal and my need for long talks to sort out thoughts, ideas and problems were not congenial to him. To add to my feelings of loneliness, we had moved to a new home in a remote, isolated area, where I was unable to find a community of like-minded spirits.

I was recovering from my car accident, which prevented for months my active engagement in work of any kind. In other words, I was immobilized, stopped in my tracks and for the first time unable to run. I fell into a deep depression. My coping mechanism became disengagement and escape from real life. For the first time in my life, I started watching soaps and reading romance novels. As my husband watched in amazement I became an avid fan of Barbara Cartland, devouring every new volume I could get my hands on. Since I was still unable to get involved with any meaningful work, I became very busy with meaningless activity, busy work.

My injuries were healing, but I was stuck in my black mood and escapism. Neither my husband nor my marriage could compete with the Regency romances absorbing my time and thoughts, and allowing me to dwell in a beautiful unreality. The fantasy of perfect love, which I so much longed for, did not find reflection in real life.

The fateful morning when I woke up with the sun streaming in the windows, its light dispelling the darkness of the previous months signaled the end of my depression. It was like waking up from a long sleep. I felt energized and ready to live again. I'm not sure how to explain the sudden lifting of the depression, which had lasted for months. I was not on any medication. From an energetic viewpoint, it was certainly a major shift. I had wallowed long enough in self-pity and helplessness and was ready to take responsibility and action once again. Perhaps, I was just bored with inaction.

My husband encouraged me strongly to pursue my interest in psychology. He believed and kept assuring me that I was intelligent and talented and should be doing something to develop my gifts. I started a practice of psychotherapy and discovered a passion for the work. New horizons kept appearing as I became more and more engaged in the study and practice. I had found my bliss. In studying psychology and psychotherapy in a deeply committed way, I started to understand and unravel some of my own problems, I started to know who I was. In studying marriage therapy, I began to gain insight into our relationship issues. Insight and understanding, by themselves, are not enough to effect change. But they are a necessary start. Without insight and understanding change is difficult to achieve. The path to healing and learning sometimes is very much alike.

Ultimately, we all want understanding, acceptance and love. Only when we have that, do we feel safe, peaceful and happy. From understanding comes acceptance, and love, but first there must be forgiveness. That is the way to healing both on a spiritual and on a psychological level. This is where the two paths converge.

My understanding gained from reading, study and therapy, helped me to face the reality of my past and present. I was finally able to face the dark. The support I received from my husband and my therapists, allowed me to face the pain of my brokenness. Though I was still a long way from acceptance and forgiveness, I started being more open to experiences, which illuminated my issues, and more receptive to clues which appeared all around me.

Getting past the enormity of my childhood losses was an important step. I was in my late-fifties when I had the following dream:

I am sitting at the gate in a large airport, waiting to board the flight to Warsaw. It's getting very late and I don't see my destination listed on the board of departures. I decide to investigate, but first make a stop in the ladies' room. Then, I check the flight information and discover that I was waiting at the wrong gate. When I finally get to the right one, the flight is already boarding. When asked for my ticket and ID, I find my purse is missing. I leave my luggage by the gate, and urged to hurry by the attendant rush back to the other gate and the ladies' room but in vain. The pocketbook is gone and with it my tickets, passport and several hundred dollars for the trip. I have lost everything and can't continue my journey.

Returning sad and depressed to the gate, I inform the attendant of what happened. She is very busy and tells me gruffly to sit and wait, grumbling about the paperwork. She tells me my luggage is already on the plane. "But I can't go," I cry out. She waives me on board explaining that she is processing my insurance, which covers such contingencies. Everything will be taken care of, and I will receive thirty thousand dollars in reimbursement.

I woke up stunned. Careful analysis of the dream over a period of time revealed many nuggets of gold, but the clear message was: I feel that having lost everything I can't continue my journey, but in reality having lost everything I have lost nothing (note the paradox). In fact, I ended up with much, much more than I had originally lost. I had this powerful dream later in life, when I was ready to hear and accept its message.

THIRTY-TWO

Forgiveness

WHEN MY YOUNG SON WAS TAKING HIS FIRST TRIP TO EUROPE, on his own, his itinerary included passage through and a stop in Germany. Pouring out all my bottled up resentment and hatred, I urged him to change his route and avoid the country of my nightmares. My son reminded me of all the great German musicians and writers, including one of his favorite poets, Rainer Maria Rilke. When I persisted with my condemnation of the entire country, he accused me of prejudice. This was a blow below the belt. I had always prided myself on having no prejudices. I rationalized that this was not a true prejudice rather a fair judgment based on atrocities the Germans had committed. But, as he pointed out, this was a new generation and it was prejudicial to hold the sons accountable for the sins of the fathers. At first, I was very angry. In time, as I pondered his position, I started questioning my attitude. Forgiving the Nazi atrocities did not seem possible -- then how far do I extend my hatred of the perpetrators? When and whom can or should any of us forgive?

A few years later, I met the son-in-law of my dear friends, who are ethnic and cultural Jews. Their son-in-law, whom I will call Kurt, is a German, born and raised in Germany. His father had been a Nazi, a member of the infamous SS. An intelligent, sensitive man, Kurt loved his Jewish wife to whom he has been happily married for many years and with whom he has two children. I found it impossible to dislike this man, or to think of him in the way I had heretofore thought of *all* Germans. Meeting and liking him caused a paradigm shift in my consciousness. I was forced to consider that not all Germans were evil. Kurt exemplifies the new generation of Germans who are appalled by the crimes against humanity committed by their parents. They carry feelings of guilt and a desire for atonement. Many have dedicated themselves to promoting non-violence and to serving causes for peace. Germany has directly apologized to Israel, and made reparations for its was crimes.

In 1951 the West German Chancellor admitted: "... *unspeakable crimes have been committed in the name of the German people, calling for moral and material indemnity ... The Federal Government are prepared, jointly with representatives of Jewry and the State of Israel ... to bring about a solution of the material indemnity problem, thus easing the way to the spiritual settlement of infinite suffering."*

The acknowledgment by perpetrators of what they have done and apology for their actions is considered a pre-requisite for forgiveness and reconciliation. But it is not always possible nor is it always enough. Forgiveness is a stumbling block for many, as it was for me. I had to forgive the violence and atrocities which I first experienced in childhood and which continued to haunt me in the present. Unjust wars, genocide, the massacre of innocents, the torture and humiliation of helpless prisoners all violated powerfully my sense of decency and justice. Forgiving the perpetrators was very, very hard, well nigh impossible.

Harder still, was forgiving myself. On a deep level there was always the guilt of the survivor. Why me? Why did I survive when so many others perished? But deeper still was the acknowledgment of my own shadow side. Although I could never, in my wildest imagination see myself engaging voluntarily in the horrific acts of cruelty which revolted and appalled me, and yet, and yet... I know from psychology that there are deeply hidden urges and dark parts of the unconscious that we are not aware of and that shock and surprise us when we get a brief glimpse. I know again from studying human nature, that given the right set of circumstances we are all capable of almost any act. I know that the monsters committing these crimes against humanity were and are, in fact as human, as I am. I also think of reincarnation. If I have lived before, is it possible that I too have committed terrible deeds?

Hannah Arendt, the brilliant philosopher who understood before most others that great evil is not perpetrated by great men and women who are evil but rather by the average, commonplace, ordinary person. Indifference, self-indulgence and self-deception lead to the amorality, which allows for atrocities and great crimes. This is one of the numerous versions of the famous statement by Lutheran pastor, Martin Niemöller:

In Germany, they came first for the Communists, And I didn't speak up because I wasn't a Communist;

And then they came for the trade unionists, And I didn't speak up because I wasn't a trade unionist;

And then they came for the Jews, And I didn't speak up because I wasn't a Jew;

And then ... they came for me ... And by that time there was no one left to speak up.

Like Hannah Arendt many years later, Niemöller understood early on that failure to stand up for others results in silent complicity, and that evil, once unleashed at others will eventually reach those who remain neutral as well. But it took much time, many years for me to be able to take that in.

And as I could not forgive Germany and Soviet Russia for the atrocities of WWII, I thought about the atrocities perpetrated by the country I now call my home, the United States. Starting with the genocide of Native American people, the killing of 250,000 innocent Philippinos, the estimates of between one and three million Vietnamese casualties in what they call the "American War', over 100,000 civilian deaths from violence in Iraq? These are just a few of the catastrophes we, as a country are directly or indirectly responsible for. And what about the atrocities we have committed? What about massacres of innocents like MyLai? What about torture and degradation like in Abu Graib, Guantanamo and many other rendition sites the public has never heard about? Don't we need forgiveness too? We are not innocent. We too, have blood on our hands.

A character in Susan Howatch's novel, *Ultimate Prizes,* muses about himself:

> *"...A good man? Outwardly, perhaps. But inwardly? And as I began to see myself as a good man capable of evil deeds, I realized the concentration camps were only a manifestation on a huge scale of the disorder, which has the power to cripple each human soul. It was all one. Evil was an ever present reality... "*

This notion of the unity of opposites is reflected in the Chinese concept of Yin and Yang. The light contains darkness and the darkness contains light. It is all one. I came across it vividly in my study of Jung. All opposites including good and evil are on a continuum, two ends of one pole. Two polarities which, when pushed to their extreme, convert to their opposite. This is the troubling concept of enantiodromia, which Jung had adopted from the pre-Socratic Greek philosopher Heraclitus. Jung described it as *" ... a psychological law which is unfailingly valid in personal affairs. ... a fundamental law of life—enantiodromia or conversion into the opposite"* and *"...the transformation of the hitherto valued into the worthless, and of the former good into the bad".* A frightening thought, that sets our linear thinking minds, fond of dualistic black and white thinking, on edge.

But the reverse is also possible. The former evil can be converted into good. The losses and trauma that I experienced through my early life left me struggling with painful consequences. They also taught me the lesson of impermanence and the value of non-attachment. The trick was to find balance, and not to end up unable to form any attachments. Though attached for a long time to my lost homeland, I was finally able to let go of the past. And, it was then, that I was able to embrace a new reality. Not having a country, not being a true national anywhere, I could belong everywhere: because, like the title of my friend, John Huddleston's book, *The World is One Country*. This is a form of thinking and experiencing the world that is inclusive rather than exclusive. Ultimately, perhaps the purpose of my suffering was to learn to love in an inclusive, non-attached way.

"If you pursue the truth far enough you always wind up in the land of paradox. You reach a point where the apparent truth divides into two opposing truths, and then you have to try to reach beyond them to grasp the ultimate truth, their synthesis" Susan Howatch, *Ultimate Prizes*.

These are difficult ideas to think about much less to accept and incorporate into our life philosophy. It is easy to see the good within us and within those we love. It is very hard to recognize and admit that evil lurks within each one of us as well. And yet, if that is true, then does it not behoove us to forgive others and ourselves as well? Difficult as it is, forgiveness is critical to healing and sometimes even survival. Forgiveness is not an emotion; it is a decision, it is a choice.

I Shall Not Hate: A Gaza Doctor's Journey, by the Palestinian doctor, Izzeldin Abuelaish, is a magnificent memoir of forgiveness. After losing his wife to leukemia, he lost three daughters and a niece when an Israeli bomb blew up his home. Another daughter was badly wounded. Deeply grieving for his dead children and angry at the injustice, Dr. Abuelaish refuses to call for revenge or sink into hatred. He calls for peace and cooperation for an understanding and acceptance, and hopes that his daughters will be *"the last sacrifice on the road to peace between Palestinians and Israelis."* He writes:

"Whom shall I hate of the Israelis…the innocent Israeli babies I bring into the world? The associates with whom I have served in hospitals in Israel? I think not."

And later, he continues:

"I shall not hate. I shall be thankful. I shall continue working. I shall hope. I shall treat the survivors. I shall act for justice."

In the last quote, Dr. Abuelaish sets out the template for healing trauma. Forgive, let go of the past that cannot be changed, move forward with positive intent into the future. His action consists of working for others (*I shall treat the survivors),* and he is dedicated to a cause larger than himself (*I shall act for justice).* By justice, here, he is referring to peace between the Israelis and Palestinians.

His ability to forgive and move ahead makes it possible for him and his remaining children to survive the horrific losses his family has experienced. Because he is not bound by hate, the need for revenge or the role of victim, he will be able to act effectively and make positive contributions to humanity. And, because he is raising his young children not to hate, they too will be able to transcend the trauma and lead the authentic lives they were destined to have.

We need to let go of the impulse to take revenge for the injustice and pain we suffered. We need to actively seek to forgive and to act in a way that will allow us to heal and transcend the trauma.

Sometimes, it is ourselves we cannot forgive. In *The Tennis Partner,* a powerful memoir of a doomed friendship, Abraham Verghese writes about the path leading his friend to destruction:

"My escape from the dark path **came from reaching out to others***…His dark path,* **his pain, created an isolation***, and pretty soon he became an island unto himself, a prisoner in a solitary cell of his own construction."*

The problem was withdrawal into isolation and a refusal or inability to respond to the many efforts of others to reach out and express concern and love. This talented tennis player with a charismatic personality, and brilliant medical student with a bright future could not forgive himself for some failure, some imperfection and so he could not accept or love himself; nor could he accept the forgiveness and healing love of others. He remained a foreigner, a stranger locked in the solitude of his inner cell. He could not face the pain and so lived in the wasteland of inauthentic existence, which could only lead to despair and destruction. We all need support of friends and loved ones, as well as the guidance of wise teachers. We cannot do it alone.

Like individuals, when traumatized nations cannot forgive, let go and find a way to move into the future leaving the past behind, their anger, hatred and endless reliving of trauma distorts their character and soul. Several generations of Jews have been affected by PTSD resulting from the Holocaust, and they have not been able to get past it. Dwelling in the past, nurturing feelings of victimhood they fear that it may happen again, and live in the fantasy that a powerful state of Israel, belonging to them alone, can and will protect them in the future. To ensure the existence and power of Israel, many have sanctioned or at least tolerated acts of terror, brutality and torture against the Palestinians.

Israel has become transformed, in the words of Avraham Burg, *"From a society that aspired to realize the dreams of its founders to a persecuted and sanctimonious nation that is easily frightened, vengeful and coercive."*

By appropriating the WWII genocide as their own,

refusing to acknowledge that millions of others suffered a brutal and tortured death in that conflict, and by rejecting the genocides of other peoples as lesser evils than their own, they have isolated themselves from participation in the larger life and healing of the world. What is so tragic is that having suffered such trauma, Jews are uniquely suited to bring the light of healing to the world, which so desperately needs it. But this cannot happen while they themselves remain in the darkness of the Shoah.

Avraham Burg is a prominent Israeli politician, son of holocaust survivors, who has spent his entire life in his beloved homeland. At some point, he became aware that Israel has taken a wrong turn and he has devoted himself to the unpopular cause of bringing that awareness to his compatriots so that a radical change can come about. He has written a controversial book entitled: *The Holocaust is Over; We Must Rise From Its Ashes.* One reviewer wrote, and I agree, that this is an important book written by a courageous man. I am a Polish Christian married to an American Jew, and the trauma of the holocaust has deeply affected me in many ways. This book was life changing for me.

The children of Israel are not taught that the Holocaust happened to millions of people of various ethnic and religious backgrounds. They don't know, or think it irrelevant that while six million Jews were killed during the war, so were six million Poles. And, they seem completely unaware of the fact that non-Jews comprised almost 50% of the population of Auschwitz from 1940-44.

Burg describes how a young Israeli girl on her visit to Poland and the extermination camps wrote in her diary: "*I was crying, and I saw a group of youngsters from abroad. They didn't look Jewish to me. What were they doing here? Why are they desecrating the holy? ... In the evening, when we sat and summed up the day's events... I said they should have no part in our Auschwitz ... Everyone agreed.*"

Had these children been taught the historical facts, they would not feel that the pain and loss experienced by others is desecrating "their" Auschwitz. What is even more troubling, though, is the fact of emotional and psychological rejection of the other and isolation of the victim. Instead of joining in empathy with all who suffered in the Holocaust, this girl is denying the agony of others and rejecting their right to mourn their dead, because her Jewish trauma was so much greater that it supersedes that of others. Claiming the Holocaust as uniquely Jewish and denying that other peoples have also suffered genocides, or diminishing their experience and trauma, isolates Jews from the rest of humanity. They are so caught up in their own pain from the past, they cannot acknowledge and respond with empathy to the trauma of others.

An Israeli reporter for the *Yediot Aharonot*, Israel's most authoritative daily newspaper, quoted a major Jewish leader in the United States:

"A day commemorating the Armenians will lead to other memorial days, to the Native Americans, Vietnamese, Irish, or any other people. It will damage the importance of Shoah Day."

Rabbi Michael Lerner, who has devoted his life to healing the Israeli-Palestinian conflict wrote about the role of trauma, and its critical importance in conflict resolution:

"Huge traumas have constricted the ability of Israelis and Palestinians to see and act upon what is in their own best interests. For those of us who truly care about the well-being of both sides, or even of either side, the task is to heal the trauma."

As I explained earlier in this book, unhealed trauma brings with it symptoms of exaggerated watchfulness and wariness, hyper-vigilance bordering and sometimes crossing into paranoia. Burg describes this vividly as the mental state of Israel:

"For us, every killing is a murder, every murder a pogrom, every terror attack an anti-Semitic act and every new enemy a Hitler. Behind every danger lurks a new holocaust. We, and many of our leaders who incite us,

believe that almost everyone wants to destroy us. By feeling so threatened by shadows that will attack us at dawn, we have become a nation of attackers. We feel good in this darkness, as we have become accustomed to it."

The "under siege" mentality is a result of the self imposed alienation and isolation. Burg correctly attributes the predicament and behavior of Israel to unhealed trauma:

"Instead of harnessing modern Jewish fortitude to repair the world and oppose its injustices, we find too many Jews that are haunted by past traumas. They cannot change and adapt, in the same way that a ship in the ocean cannot come to a full stop in less than a few miles. Diaspora Jews, including many of their representatives, choose the side of authority and become partners in the world's injustices and insensitivities."

He explains the path to healing: we must leave the past behind and take on the responsibilities of the present: "repair, redemption, restoration and reconstruction of the ruins". That is moving forward into a future of hope and freedom rather than remaining stuck in the chains of past despair. Safety for Israel will not come from building fences to keep others out, it will come from opening its doors and hearts to others (the stranger) and embracing them in brotherly love. It is only then that Israel will become a true part of the brotherhood of nations not as a paranoid victim of past atrocities, but as an equal partner worthy of respect and support.

"Israel must leave Auschwitz, because Auschwitz is a mental prison. Life inside the camp is survival laced with guilt and victimology; life outside the camp is of constant alarm. Auschwitz and its chimneys are lighthouses to guide us toward a better moral and humanistic life, not a point into which all our life's ships sail and crash. I believe with all my heart that when Israel frees itself from its obsession with the Shoah and its exclusivity, the world also will be much freer."

"The most important Jewish legacy is to assume responsibility for repair, redemption, restoration, and reconstruction of the ruins."

Burg leaves us with the hope for a better future, if we can heal and leave the past behind.

"We are fast approaching an intersection where we need decide who we are and where we are going. Are we going to the past, toward which we always oriented ourselves, or will we choose the future, for the first time in generations? Will we choose a better world that is based on hope and not trauma, on trust in humanity and not suspicious isolationism and paranoia? In this case we will have to leave our pain behind us and look forward, to find out where we can repair ourselves and perhaps even the world."

THIRTY-THREE

Opening the Heart: Reconciliation

"... *Healing has to be as radical and complex as the wound and hurt. Any realistic assessment of what thorough, long term healing means in a world like ours must talk about costly and risky processes 'Clinical interventions' have their place, but they deal with a very limited range of problems. If deep suffering and evil could be dealt with by formulas, techniques, and a problem-solving mentality, then our civilization above all should have been able to make progress in coping with war, poverty, debt, violence, addiction, family breakup, injustice, and a multitude of other evils and miseries that fill the media.*" The Shape of Living-David F. Ford

This brings me to the final crucial and perhaps most difficult part of the journey: acceptance and opening of the heart to others. Without an open heart there can be no exchange of life-giving love. With a closed heart, one cannot give or receive love. The concept of radical hospitality, inclusiveness and acceptance is key to the healing of our wounds. As Burg suggests, Israel needs to shed its exclusivity and isolationism and espousing instead the inclusiveness and acceptance of the rest of humanity in order to heal and become the positive force in the world it can be. This applies to individuals as well. *The Tennis Player* remained in isolation, unable to open his heart, and he died in isolation without contributing any of his many valuable gifts to the world. Many factors went into my final ability to let go of my exclusive pain and open my heart to embracing others.

In my journey of healing, I learned that the purpose of my suffering was to learn the necessary lessons, so that I could fully become who I was meant to be: a truly loving being. I needed to learn to love in a non-attached way. The beautiful prayer attributed to St. Francis spoke powerfully to me:

> O, Divine Master, grant that I may not so
>   much seek
> To be consoled, as to console,
> To be understood, as to understand,
> To be loved, as to love
> For it is in giving that we receive…

This prayer spoke to my heart and helped me grasp, finally, that this was not all about me. That it was not about me at all, but rather all about others. Opening of the heart to embrace the 'Other', leads to reconciliation not only with those who have hurt us, but, significantly with our inner selves as well. It frees us to find and dedicate ourselves to our own deep and true purpose, to a goal larger than ourselves.

THIRTY-FOUR

Dedication To Higher Goal

"But what is wanted is a worthy object to which the individual can devote his whole energies, which shall grip and unify and inspire; only as he can see and occupy himself in relation to a single large purpose will he find peace and power." Charles E. Raven, *"The Creator Spirit"*

This "worthy object" will be different for each person. Everyone has their own, unique purpose and destiny. For me, realizing the purpose of my life was service to others. That was my dedication to a goal larger than myself. For others it may be music, art, a worthy cause, a relationship or something else. What matters is discovering our own true path. Travelling the path of another, leads to the tragedy of an inauthentic and unfulfilled life.

Alchemy is the process of transforming a base metal into gold. The long, painful process of healing trauma is alchemical in nature as it transforms the person who perseveres through to the end of the journey. It has transformed my life.

In my childhood, I lived through the chaos and conflagration of war. My world went up in flames. I existed during my childhood and adolescence in a landscape devastated by fire, filled with scorched dreams and the ashes of an aborted future. In my young adulthood, I tried to rebuild, I tried to build a fairy castle on top of all the ashes. But ashes are not a strong foundation on which to build, and the castle collapsed.

An epic fire always leaves destruction in its wake. Still, in time nature always comes back. The land is healed, trees and plants grow again. Those trees that have survived the destruction, after the initial shock grow stronger. The ashes get absorbed into the earth and nourish the soil. The earth is the key. It is the ground, the foundation out of which healthy growth can spring forth.

I worked hard throughout my life digging in the soil of my inner being, trying to rebuild the solid foundation that had been destroyed in my childhood years. All that work prepared me for the psychic breakthrough, when I was finally able to let go of the trauma, of the pain and move on towards healing. For me, God is the ground of my being, the rock solid foundation on which I can build with security.

For some people, their foundation is family, home, society, work. The problem with such foundations is that they are temporary. They are all capable of being lost. Only that, which is permanent within us, is that which we can always depend on being there. We must all find some foundation within, before we can have the security required to take the risks necessary in the pursuit of our authentic journey through life. Once we have established our foundation, we can then proceed to investigate who we are, discovering our true self and finally our purpose/goals in life.

Does this mean that I am now always happy and content, bringing light and love to all around me? No. I remain an imperfect human working consciously to continue on the path of transformation and healing. But having shed most of my chains, I am able to move ahead instead of running around in circles. I see clearly my path forward. And, while my burden is not light, it is much, much lighter. There is much more work for me to do, but I feel confident that I will have the resources needed to do it. I am happier and more content than ever before.

I believe that through our own personal transformation and healing, we can transform and heal our traumatized world and planet. Today, we are facing a future of great darkness, which threatens to envelop the entire world and even wipe out life, as we know it. Despite the very real danger and threat of destruction, I believe that, in the words of Chris Hedges, love will endure.

"The power of love is greater than the power of death. It cannot be controlled. It is about sacrifice for the other-something nearly every parent understands-rather than exploitation. It is about honoring the sacred. And power elites have for millennia tried and failed to crush the force of love. Blind and dumb, indifferent to the siren calls of celebrity, unable to bow before illusions, defying the lust for power, love constantly rises up to remind a wayward society of what is real and what is illusion. Love will endure, even if it appears darkness has swallowed us all, to triumph over the wreckage that remains." - Hedges, *Empire of Illusion*.

Afterword

This book is the story of my journey in search of healing. Everyone engaged in the journey of life will face suffering sooner or later, in one form or another. As the Buddha said, all life is suffering. How we deal with it and emerge on the other side enriched rather than impoverished by the experience is what matters. Suffering is an inescapable part of life.

I have outlined the stages that I found essential to the process of healing. First, always, is facing the pain: facing the reality of what is. Denial of one's own pain leads to a life rooted in unreality. It also leads to a lack of empathy, to the dismissal of the suffering of others. Next, is the difficult process of letting go. It involves understanding and empathy, the ability to relate one's suffering to that of others, which then opens us to compassion and forgiveness. Finally, it means a re-orientation from looking back, dwelling on the unchangeable past, to looking forward to the future, which is ours to forge. It means making a commitment to that future. This involves discovering who we really are and the purpose of our life: what it is that gives it meaning. Understanding leads to forgiveness, forgiveness opens the heart to love and allows us to find that higher goal worthy of our commitment and dedication.

We each have our own path, our own destiny. We each have our own talents, which we can use to enrich our lives and those of others. Unless we discover the unique blueprint for our life, as long as we live someone else's dream instead of our own, we will be doomed to an unfulfilled, inauthentic existence.

The specifics are different for each individual. For example, I have the gift of connecting with people lost in their suffering and the ability to help guide them out of their wasteland. I am eternally grateful for this gift. Using it to benefit others gives me a great sense of fulfillment. Another person may find fulfillment in making beautiful music or art. Someone else by fighting for justice, protecting the weak, feeding the poor, or creating jobs. The list is endless.

The Buddha also said that suffering is caused by attachment. The many painful losses I had experienced in my life brought home to me the truth of that statement. The same losses also taught me, that everything in life is transient and impermanent; everything is liable to change and disappear. The natural first response to such a frightening scenario was, for me, a closing of the heart and emotions, which only increased the pain of insecurity and loneliness. It took me many years to discover the secret of healing. It is radical hospitality: keeping the heart open to everything. Grasping this concept is difficult, accepting and implementing it even more so, yet it is critical. It is expressed beautifully, in a poem by William Blake:

> "He who binds himself to a joy,
> Does the winged life destroy.
> But he, who kisses the joy as it flies
> Lives in Eternity's sunrises."

A final point. As I state in the book, for me, God is the ground of my being. Not everyone will or must come to such a conclusion. But to become whole, everyone must find his or their own center that can hold, the ground of their being. This book was written for all those suffering from unhealed trauma. My hope in writing it was to provide some guideposts for travellers struggling on the difficult path of healing. If it has given hope and help to even one reader, it will have achieved its purpose and given me fulfillment and joy.

Dear reader,

We hope you enjoyed reading *A Child of War*. Please take a moment to leave a review, even if it's a short one. Your opinion is important to us.

Discover more books by Ewa Hammer at https://www.nextchapter.pub/authors/ewa-hammer

Want to know when one of our books is free or discounted? Join the newsletter at http://eepurl.com/bqqB3H

Best regards,

Ewa Hammer and the Next Chapter Team

You might also like:
The Last Tiger by Tony Black

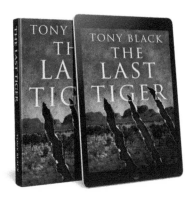

To read the first chapter for free, head to:
https://www.nextchapter.pub/books/the-last-tiger

Notes

1. The War

1. In Poland, as in most European countries, Scouting was not just for children but rather a lifelong commitment to certain values and lifestyle. Scouts were pledged to serve God and Country with their 'entire' life. In times of crisis, scouts of all ages including young adolescents and children participated actively in service. In 1919, when Ukrainians attacked the city of Lvov, scouts as young as 11 and 12 years of age fought and died in its defense. They are known in Polish history as the Lvov Eaglets. At the entrance to the Old City of Warsaw, there is a monument to a 12-year old boy in helmet and holding a machine gun. He died there defending his city.

5. A Train Ride to Nowhere

1. Explanatory Note: After the surrender of Warsaw, the Germans had decided to systematically destroy the city block by block with tanks. Meanwhile they shipped out the entire population. Able-bodied men and women unencumbered by small children were sent to work camps in Germany. That is where my nanny went. Others were sent to the closest death camp, Auschwitz, for extermination. My parents separated, each holding one child, and they both ended up, as they had hoped on the same train. We were on our way to Auschwitz. Unfortunately for the Germans, the crematoria could not keep up with the hundreds of thousands of people being fed to them day and night. While the backup grew, the Soviet troops were finally starting to move, and the Germans ran out of time. They were forced to retreat before they could get our shipment to Auschwitz. As the soldiers withdrew, we were finally released from the freight car in which we were trapped, into a field. The closest village, Milanowek, was a few kilometers away, and the freed passengers, some of whom were very young, others old, sick, or barely alive, had to somehow make their way there.

26. Searching for Meaning

1. Some might question the word 'loving' used in this context. Yet it is the right word. Anyone who has ever worked in a therapeutic relationship with

another human being will recognize that without an opening of the heart to engage the other in a loving exchange, healing cannot occur.

It is a two-way transaction. The patient must have enough trust in the therapist to open up completely in a way that leaves them completely vulnerable. Such an act of trust is a great gift and a great responsibility. Only the most gentle and loving touch can be tolerated without disaster. But that loving touch is the beginning of the healing process. It is the first injection of penicillin into the infected wound, which stops the spiral of disease and initiates recovery. It can only happen when both the patient and therapist allow their open hearts to connect for an instant. In that infinitesimal moment, there comes a realization of unity. There are no longer two separate people, there is just one. So there can no longer be a question of being unwanted, abandoned or betrayed. For that brief moment, we are safe. That moment of unity, participated in equally by both parties is an act of love.

In *The Wounded Healer*, Henri Nouwen says that to effect healing, the healer must be willing to open to the other as a fellow human being with the same wounds and suffering. We heal from our own wounds. Only someone who has been wounded, can truly understand and heal another wounded being. I do not mean intellectually, with the brain, but emotionally with the heart and gut.

A Child Of War
ISBN: 978-4-86747-000-8

Published by
Next Chapter
1-60-20 Minami-Otsuka
170-0005 Toshima-Ku, Tokyo
+818035793528

13th May 2021

Lightning Source UK Ltd.
Milton Keynes UK
UKHW012144270521
384511UK00001B/121